Invincible Spirit

Invincible Spirit

JONATHAN'S JOURNEY

LIZ WICKINS

PENGUIN BOOKS

PENGUIN BOOKS

Published by the Penguin Group
80 Strand, London WC2R 0RL, England
Penguin Putnam Inc, 375 Hudson Street, New York, New York 10014,
USA
Penguin Books Australia Ltd, Ringwood, Victoria, Australia
Penguin Books Canada Ltd, 10 Alcorn Avenue, Toronto, Ontario,
Canada M4V 3B2
Penguin Books (NZ) Ltd, Cnr Rosedale and Airborne Roads, Albany,
Auckland, New Zealand
Penguin Books India (P) Ltd, 11 Community Centre, Panchsheel Park,
New Delhi – 110 017, India
Penguin Books (South Africa) (Pty) Ltd, 24 Sturdee Avenue, Rosebank,
Johannesburg 2196, South Africa

Penguin Books (South Africa) (Pty) Ltd, Registered Offices:
Second Floor, 90 Rivonia Road, Sandton 2196, South Africa

First published by Penguin Books (South Africa) (Pty) Ltd 2003

Copyright © Liz Wickins
All rights reserved
The moral right of the author has been asserted

ISBN 0 143 02423 X

Typeset by CJH Design in 10.5 on 13.5 Palatino
Cover reproduction: Mouse Design
Printed and bound by Interpak Books, KwaZulu-Natal

Except in the United States of America, this book is sold subject to the
condition that it shall not, by way of trade or otherwise, be lent, resold,
hired out or otherwise circulated without the publisher's prior consent
in any form of binding or cover other than that in which it is published
and without a similar condition including this condition being imposed
on the subsequent purchaser.

Dedicated to all invincible spirits
but particularly Jonathan's

Acknowledgements

Many of my friends and family believed that I could write our story successfully and I am grateful to them for their faith in me, and the encouragement that was forthcoming. My sisters urged and supported me throughout the process, particularly my sister Pat in Australia, who read each chapter as it was finished and put pressure on me to send the next – she was that certain that I could do it. Her husband Michael assured me that 'Wickins was not Dickens' but the honesty in relating the story made up for it. I am indebted to my sister Cath, whose judgement and knowledge of books I hugely respect, and who spent hour upon hour working with me during the initial edit, helping me choose just the right words.

I am grateful to Lord Rix for endorsing this project by writing the foreword. It means a great deal to me, given his position and personal experience with Down syndrome.

I thank Penguin South Africa, particularly the CEO Alison Lowry for deciding to publish *Invincible Spirit*, and Jane Ranger for her commitment to the cause and very hard work as the editor.

Most of all, I thank my immediate family for allowing themselves to be exposed in this way. To Barry, for once again supporting me in a challenge, the way he always has, and to Jonny and Graeme for giving me this story to share.

Foreword by Lord Rix CBE DL
President of Mencap (UK)

In the course of a long career in the theatre and the world of disability, you tend to attract honours of various sorts – from invitations to open things to honorary degrees. Having a seat in the Upper House of the Westminster Parliament, and the right to speak up for disabled people and their families, comes high on this list of special opportunities. However, quite the most heart-warming honour is to be 'invited into someone's family': to write the foreword to their family story. I do so as the father of an adult daughter with Down (or Down's) syndrome and the grandfather of a young boy (my son's boy) with Down syndrome.

Liz Wickins captures very well the unique perspectives of mother, father, siblings, and the person with a learning disability himself, in a family with a disabled member. Sometimes those perspectives coincide. Sometimes they don't. In a book with a number of memorable phrases, I particularly liked the description of this family experience as having 'pictures in their minds and the burn holes in their hearts'.

Each child with Down syndrome is different. Each family member reacts and interacts differently. People laugh, cry, cope and triumph in their own, and sometimes in unexpected, ways. The wider family and the wider community can help or hinder; and the immediate family may be concerned a lot, a little or not at all by the way others behave towards their child. As the author says, children and adults with learning disabilities can create a helpful learning experience for others – with the parents and siblings as more or less willing participants.

This story is set in South Africa, and describes a white family fairly well provided with material resources. The experience of a black family in different material circumstances with a Down syndrome child would in many respects be very different. However, I suspect that the two families would also have a lot in common – united by shared experience of a disability which cuts across ethnic and economic differences. I have to use the term disability, but a very important part of the big ethical debate about 'prevention' of Down syndrome is the reality that – as with Jonathan – people with Down syndrome tend to have certain personal characteristics which we all value. Without those characteristics, our world would be a much poorer place.

I read with particular interest the descriptions of encounters with professionals. The good and bad are all laid out here. There is the professional who sees disability as a failure of possibilities – which puts the disabled person into a low priority second class citizen category. There is the professional who sees the defects and not the person. There is the professional who has all the answers from the written book, and can't be bothered to open and read the 'person book'. At the same time, there are professionals who value the disabled person for who they are, and give equality of status, and are quite happy to sweat blood for a little progress.

It is possible to ignore hostile or indifferent neighbours or strangers. It is quite hard to ignore the professional who for the moment has the ability to influence for good or ill your son or daughter's life. This is why I have devoted a good deal of my energy to getting the professionals 'on board'. Doctors, nurses, teachers, therapists, and other professionals could do worse than read this book and take to heart the lasting effects of poor attitudes and the abiding memory of good attitudes.

Brian Rix

Introduction

I have always believed that everything that happens in our lives, happens for a particular reason. At the time we seldom acknowledge that there is a purpose, because the need to change is often unwelcome and can be painful. Only in retrospect do the choices we've made and the consequences of those choices become clear and add dimension to our lives.

This book is about a family who have had to adapt their lives to include a boy with Down syndrome, with all its challenges and joys. His name is Jonathan and the family is mine. The experience has changed our attitudes forever and I hope that telling you about it will change yours. If only a handful of people benefit from what I have to share, the aim and purpose of the book will have been realised and the significance of Jonathan's life will be more meaningful than it already is.

Our experiences as a family are not always unique to Down syndrome, and could quite often also apply to other mental disabilities. One of my objectives in writing this book is to share with others the dynamics of coping with a child like Jonathan who has been plagued, until now, with ill health. There have been a number of books written about children with Down syndrome which have romanticised and even fictionalised the sometimes harsh realities. My aim is to tell our story exactly as it happened, the good and the bad.

If such a thing as a 'run-of-the-mill' or textbook case of Down syndrome exists, Jonathan is not one of them. The word 'syndrome' indicates common characteristics and although Jonathan has all the typical features, his ways of developing and learning are unique. What you read about Jonathan or our reaction to him should not be applied to other children with Down syndrome or their families. This is our story, our emotions. As I wrote these pages, I became aware that new parents of a child with Down syndrome may feel threatened, thinking this is what they have to look forward to. We have been unfortunate in that Jonathan has not been as well as most other children. However, many of his illnesses have not been related to Down syndrome at all.

There aren't many books available that attempt to make others understand what it actually feels like to have a child with a disability. I would have liked to have been given a book that gave me hope and just enough knowledge when Jonathan was born – something to cling to until the beautiful relationship with him had developed and none of the medical information mattered anymore. That's where we are now. Jonathan is no longer someone with Down syndrome; he is Jonathan. A long time ago we stopped asking the questions we had initially asked: 'How, why, what now?' It was important then, but not anymore.

There is a strong underlying message in our story and I hope it remains clear. More important than the hard times them-selves, are the lessons you take from them. Without

Jonathan, we would have missed some fundamental lessons reminding us that there's more to life than personal perfection.

My husband Barry insisted that I not spare his feelings when describing his early reaction to Jonathan's birth. By leaving out his initial sadness and rejection, we would have nothing against which to measure his subsequent joy and unconditional acceptance. I will always be proud of his honesty and courage in recounting his first reactions and emotions, and his subsequent unswerving support and love.

Although the story starts before Jonathan was born, it's integrally linked to my circumstances at the time, so I've devoted the first chapter to recounting the decade prior to his birth.

Today it seems we are living in times where we need to know more about everything, including Down syndrome. This interest has evoked questions and hopefully the interest will last so that people with Down syndrome are better understood. It is a personal joy for me to see people with Down syndrome in public places, a less common sight twenty years ago. The more they are seen, the more questions will be asked. I know that Jonathan has changed the thinking of many of my friends because of the contact they've had with him. I'm very proud of that and consider it my contribution towards bridging the awareness gap, no matter how minuscule. These small successes have encouraged me to try and bridge that gap on a larger scale – hence this book.

I hope to try and change some common misconceptions and bring readers closer to the joy these children experience and the joy they bring to others. There is always sadness connected with the birth of a child with a disability. However, as is in the case in dealing with grief, there is often a recognisable process before acceptance and unconditional love prevail, which they invariably do.

I hope you will find answers to questions you have been too afraid to ask, such as:

Does one congratulate the new parents of a child with a disability?

Does one sympathise with them?

What should one write in the card one sends them – 'I'm pleased' or 'I'm sorry'?

People with Down syndrome are unique and it is a mistake to group them together and consider them the same because they look alike. They are alike in that they have similar physical characteristics and some common personality traits, but they are as individual as you and I. Because they have a syndrome, there is no reason not to try to understand them as individuals and treat them with the dignity and respect they deserve.

The calm that has come over me in recent times has made the writing of this story possible. It has been an unexpectedly cathartic undertaking, bringing again to the surface almost forgotten traumas and joys, allowing me to revisit and lay to rest unresolved issues from the past.

I have written it chronologically and hope you will find the patience to bear with me through the hard times, knowing that there are better days to share with you.

I have two children, although the focus of this book rests mainly on one of them, Jonathan, because his condition is the subject of my writing. Graeme is as important to us as Jonathan, and I hope that this book will make it evident that Graeme is as remarkable a person as his brother.

I leave it to you, the reader, to decide whether the invincible spirit is Jonathan's alone or the collective invincible spirit of the family unit.

This is our story.

Chapter 1

I was thirty-two years old and at a stage where many thirty-two-year-olds find themselves: married, the mother of a three-year-old child and expecting a second child. A series of dramatic and at times traumatic events, spanning a decade, had brought me to this time in my life.

My father, who I had been extremely close to, had died ten years previously; a loss I thought I'd never overcome. The resulting emotional chaos was compounded by a disappointing romance that had left me alone at the altar and angry at the world. I decided to transfer to the London office of the company I was working for at the time. With a heavy heart and a tight budget, I booked my passage and sailed alone to Southampton. My work permit stated the reason for my visit was to 'study English business methods'. It looked impressive, but would probably have been better described as 'healing a grieving heart' or 'in search of acceptance'. I returned a few years later, having gained valuable work experience and my inner turmoil was quelled. The journey had made me see the world differently; I had made lifelong friends in England and returned ready to trust again. I was twenty-five years old and had grown up and survived what I thought was the worst thing that would ever happen to me.

However, fate intervened and I changed my job soon after my return from England. This was when I met my husband Barry. One day I looked up from my desk and Barry was standing in the corridor outside the glass partition of my office. The team of auditors had arrived and he was in charge of them. He looked as if he belonged on a rugby field, not in an office, and the files he was carrying under his arm could've been the ball. It turned out to be the happiest audit I have ever worked on.

With no doubt or hesitation, we were married on my twenty-sixth birthday. It was always the big events that brought home the loss of my father, and it is still an ongoing sadness for me that he and Barry never met. My mother has always believed that I was attracted to Barry because he is so much like my father. Both gentle men of great physical and moral stature.

Being newly married comes with challenges, and ours was no different. To add to the challenge, I had started experiencing blinding headaches. They plagued the early years of our marriage, requiring frequent hospitalisation and endless tests that never provided us with any answers or solutions. Through a haze of pain and medication, life carried on until I got a call from my doctor's receptionist to say the neurologist wanted to see us. A pituitary tumour had been found to be the cause of the headaches, and the initial treatment was to take medication for six months in an attempt to shrink it. This had no effect and it was then decided to remove the tumour surgically. That's the only time in my life I remember being completely paralysed by fear. I was sitting at the hospital admissions desk and I know it was paralysis, because if I could have moved, I would have run. I must have looked terrified, because the admissions clerk said, 'Don't worry, dear, they won't shave your hair off.' It was not my hair I was worried about, it was my life!

The operation was harrowing, but nevertheless successful and we were assured that the tumour had definitely needed to be removed. I froze when I heard the doctor tell Barry, 'I needed to remove most of the gland which means you probably won't be able to have children, but it was that or probable blindness.' The invasive headaches had robbed me of three years of my life and now threatened to change my life forever. No children! This was an eventuality that neither of us had ever considered. I was discharged, but returned a number of times to have infections around the operation site cleared. Meanwhile, the headaches persisted.

They got worse in the year that followed with migraine after migraine, one often striking before the previous one had even dissipated. This meant more time in hospital, more drips and more medication. I then took a turn for the worse and was hospitalised, a drip was set up and tests were run. I felt as if my life was over when, in fact, my life was actually just beginning. Imagine my surprise and delight when the test results revealed that I was pregnant. If I had known it was possible, I would have been far more conscious of what medication I had been taking.

Graeme was born a healthy little boy. Because of the medication I had been given during the first trimester of my pregnancy, I had been concerned about his well-being. A miniature Barry entered the world on his father's birthday and my most vivid memory of that day was the look on Barry's face as I came round from the anaesthetic. Graeme's birth was one of the greatest highlights of his life. I am sure it is instinctive that a mother's first words after having a baby are 'Is the baby all right?' I asked this even before I knew whether he was a boy or a girl. Graeme was in an incubator and I was only able to see him for the first time once his body temperature stabilised after a few hours. I asked Barry which one of us Graeme looked like and although I drifted off to sleep immediately after his reply, his answer will always be etched in my mind. He could hardly form the words around the grin: 'He's just like me.'

How was I to know when I looked at my precious child for the first time that he was going to be so extraordinary? I'm certain every mother looks at her first baby and marvels at the miracle of life, and I was convinced that only I could produce such perfection.

Graeme became the centre of our world; he was a clever little boy with a sunny and uncomplicated nature. His first year was enthralling, watching him reach milestones and develop into a little person who reflected our values and norms. At the same time motherhood was exhausting. He was diagnosed as clinically hyperactive and never really respected the fact that nights were meant for sleeping. The whispers at mothers' teas were: 'Is your child sleeping through the night?' 'Yes, is yours?' You just needed to look around the room and spot the mothers with dark rings under their eyes to get some real answers. I was one of them. Graeme soon started to walk and talk and thrilled us every day. But we never lost sight of the fact that we may not have had this pleasure if the doctor who removed the tumour had been correct in his prognosis that we would never have children of our own.

It appeared that the stalk of the pituitary gland, which had been left behind, had taken over the function of the gland. Through these years of bliss my headaches persisted. Chronic pain is a strange thing; you become used to it. Maybe the pain doesn't change, but your tolerance of it certainly does. It really depends on what else you are dealing with at the same time. When there are other stresses in your life, the tolerance level is exceeded and that results in a crisis. These crises were not simply increased pain experiences for me, but involved pacing, throwing up, crying, rocking and falling asleep in a sitting position with a bowl on my lap, because getting to the bathroom was far too strenuous a task in my condition. If the intensity of pain could be measured on a scale of one to ten, my headache crises scored a full, bell-ringing ten.

I was getting some respite during the severe attacks by way of an anti-inflammatory injection that brought temporary relief. The intention was to break the pain cycle in the hope that it would disturb the regular pattern of the attacks, which appeared to be cyclical and hormonally linked.

One afternoon, when Graeme was two and a half years old, one of my episodes started to develop. By the time Barry returned from work in the late afternoon, my condition had deteriorated so badly that he immediately took me to the hospital.

Unbeknown to us, fate was about to strike a vicious blow.

On admission I was taken to a procedure room, where the usual anti-inflammatory injection was dispensed intra-venously into the inner elbow of my right arm. The procedure

10

room had become familiar to me as I had been there several times under the same circumstances, and always arrived unable to walk unaided from the car.

Usually, I would feel the effect of the medication very soon after it was injected but this time I didn't. Instead I felt an intense pain in my right hand and the doctor quietly said, 'Move your fingers.' The pain in my head had already rendered me dysfunctional and with the additional pain in my hand, I was unable to make reliable judgements as to what was happening around me. I was also confused by the activity in the room, with doctors rushing in and out, looking flustered and whispering to one another behind their hands.

I was then taken to the X-ray department, where a catheter was inserted via the artery in my right groin and fed into my arm in an attempt to dissolve a clot that had formed in my wrist. Some of the anti-inflammatory medication had finally found its way to my head, and I started to have some fairly lucid thoughts for the first time. Strangely enough, it occurred to me that I should have shaved my legs – a thought probably brought on by the numerous male doctors crowding around my bed. Vanity, thy name is woman!

I needed to use the bathroom and was taken to the one in the intensive care unit. I assumed that I had been taken there because it was the closest, never dreaming that the ICU would be my home for the next few weeks.

I clambered back onto the bed and was mildly surprised when it was pushed into the ICU. Barry had been waiting downstairs for me, expecting me to be ready to go home at any minute. He was called up to the ICU and as he

11

approached my bed, a doctor he didn't know walked up to him and introduced himself. 'Your wife has had the blood flow to her right hand cut off for more than half an hour, so we are looking at partial paralysis, paralysis or even amputation.' Shocked and confused, I looked at Barry, and his face confirmed that I had not misheard what the doctor had said. His devastated expression still haunts me.

Things are far more settled in our lives today and I often mull over important incidents that Barry and I needed to share. Not only the good times, but times that have created the opportunities to forge unbreakable bonds. Not all couples have moments that create these bonds.

After a few weeks of intense anxiety, my right forearm was amputated just below the elbow. Something had gone terribly wrong with the administration of the injection and gangrene had set in a few days later, resulting in a mutilated limb and a battered psyche. Subsequent legal action and settlement preclude me from discussing this matter further.

Once the amputation had healed and the dreaded therapy sessions had come to an end, I was able to get on with my life. Things gradually returned to normal with the help of my family, particularly my sister Margaret, who put her life in Australia on hold in order to support me. Obviously, I was subject to bouts of deep frustration and melancholy, but the ability of the human spirit to adapt and assimilate drastic new circumstances is almost infinite. Life stops for no one and I was no exception. I soon settled into my new life, blissfully unaware of the series of calamities that were about to unfold.

I had to learn to write using my left hand, just one of the

countless frustrations and challenges related to losing an upper limb. I was fitted with a prosthetic arm, but I chose not to wear it because I found I was more functional without it. Graeme was young enough to accept the change in my appearance and in true Graeme fashion, it didn't make a difference to him. Some of his nursery school friends, when he was about four years old, taunted him saying that his mother had no arm. He indignantly retorted, 'Oh yes, she does! It's in her bedroom cupboard.'

Barry has always been a man with a clear agenda. He has a career which comes with its own challenges, but has always managed to balance the responsibilities of work with home. Barry is a man whose happiness is dependent on the well-being and security of his family, making him fiercely protective and vulnerable if any of us are hurt in any way.

I have noticed frequently how Barry, quietly, without fuss or drawing attention to the fact, helps me in social situations. Often, when we're out for dinner he stands next to me at the table and cuts my food into manageable pieces, without anybody noticing, before he thinks of his own meal. He's never complained about attending to the cutlery difficulties of two family members, while his own food gets cold, and has risen to these challenges so well.

I'm lucky that Barry didn't have access to a crystal ball before our marriage as I have no doubt that he would have made a dash for it, never to be seen again.

Chapter 2

A year lapsed between losing my arm and falling pregnant with my second child. Although it was soon after the amputation, the pregnancy was planned as I wanted to get all hospital matters in my life over with. I hoped I'd never see the inside of a hospital again after the birth of my baby. How wrong I was! I knew that I was pregnant within four weeks of conception because of the severe vomiting that started and continued unabated for the ensuing seven months.

Because I had been worried about Graeme's well-being when I was carrying him, and all my fears had been unfounded when he was born perfectly healthy, I was lulled into a false sense of security during my second pregnancy. I can't say I even considered the possibility of a problem with the pregnancy. I had the routine scans and the pregnancy developed normally, other than a few concerns towards the end that the baby was not moving as much as expected. I would sometimes arrive at the doctor's rooms, without an appointment, and ask the sister to listen for the baby's heartbeat to reassure me that all was well, something a number of expectant mothers do. I had vomited so much in the seventh month that I had become severely dehydrated and my levels of potassium were depleted.

'You'll be fine,' the gynaecologist told me at one of my weekly visits. 'The dates look right; I think you have about five weeks to go, so that takes us to the end of April.' He seemed pleased because my due date happened to slot in perfectly with his planned Easter holiday.

The baby's room was ready and waiting for the imminent arrival. I had shopped carefully for a suitably smart 'welcome home' outfit for the baby and finally settled on a gorgeous little white, velvety suit – not blue or pink for obvious reasons, but also not yellow or green in case the baby was jaundiced. Yellow or green does not go with a jaundiced complexion!

It was a Saturday afternoon and we had taken Graeme to an Easter fair. We strolled among the stalls and as I stood waiting for Barry, who had gone in search of a toilet with Graeme, I felt a sudden, transient cramp. I thought the baby was telling me to get off my feet so we left the fair and went home. It had been planned that, because of my history, I would have a Caesarean section delivery. I had not had any experience of labour pains during my first pregnancy, so I did not recognise the strange sensations I was having as labour pains. I had not given labour any thought because it was never in the plan that I would need to. We tucked Graeme into bed and later that night I realised that they were not cramps I was experiencing, but labour pains. Barry phoned the doctor only to hear what we already knew and had forgotten – he was away for the Easter holidays. We threw some things into a case and as I was closing it I remembered the special little white outfit. I ran to the baby's room, ripped it out of the chest of drawers and packed it in the bag. We had to wake Graeme and bundle him into the car before setting off for the hospital.

So this was what labour was like. The doctor who was going to deliver my baby was informed by the hospital staff via phone of my progress and they were instructed to keep me comfortable for the night with pethidine. Barry and Graeme went home and I spent the night drifting in and out of sleep, dreaming in technicolour and wondering what the next day was going to bring. A doctor I had never met before visited me early the next morning and everything started to swing into action. He yelled at one of the sisters, 'Have you phoned the father? I'm taking her in now.' I don't know how he thought Barry was going to get there in time, but by good fortune rather than good management, Barry arrived just in time to wish me good luck as I was wheeled past him in the corridor into the operating theatre.

Barry and I had decided a long time before that we wanted two children, irrespective of gender. I had spoken to the stand-in gynaecologist and he had agreed to do a sterilisation procedure at the same time as the birth. Barry waited outside the door of the operating theatre. He was not given the choice to be present at the birth because of the anaesthetic procedure. The neonatal ward was adjacent to the operating theatre and when the baby was born he was taken there to be checked by the paediatrician, Dr Judd.* Some time passed before anyone even acknowledged Barry's presence in the passageway.

'Come through here,' Dr Judd eventually said to Barry. 'What do you think of your son?'

'Another little boy!' Barry said, with a smile on his face. A

---

* Name has been changed.

16

little confused about the question, he answered, 'He's lovely.'

'But, what do you think of him? Does something look wrong?' the doctor repeated.

'He's just like his brother,' Barry replied.

'Does he look funny?'

'No, he looks just like Graeme.'

'Well, I think he has Down syndrome, but we'll have to run more tests.'

Barry was stunned. He had little idea what Down syndrome actually was. He later told me he felt like a cold hand had clutched at his heart. What about Liz? How is she going to take this and how is she going to cope?, were some of his chaotic thoughts. Confused and shocked, and staring at Jonathan for signs that it could all be a mistake, he was brought back to reality by Dr Judd saying, 'I would consider institutionalising this child. Oh, and don't tell your wife yet, I'll see you both to talk to tomorrow when she's recovered from the anaesthetic.'

He walked away and Barry stood there for a few seconds, battling with the reality of the moment. How cruel that we were not together to cope with this life-altering event. Jonathan was whisked away by the staff and Barry left the neonatal ward to take up position in the corridor, awaiting my exit from the operating theatre.

The word 'funny' has always bothered me. I'm sure it was

more related to the doctor's choice of an adjective than how Jonathan actually looked. Perhaps this was when my fierce protectiveness of Jonathan was born.

The first thing I was aware of as I came round was being wheeled out of the operating theatre and Barry walking alongside my bed.

'Is the baby all right?' I asked.

'Yes, he's fine,' Barry replied, grappling with the decision to keep the truth from me.

My face must have expressed the joy of having another precious son. I was so wrapped up in the moment, I can't say I noticed whether Barry's face was showing the same joy. He sat down next to my bed once we were in the ward. Previous hospital experiences had led me to expect him to sit with me, hold my hand and wet my lips with ice until I was settled, before he left. I had presented him with a fine son, and lay back waiting to be pampered and spoilt, basking in the knowledge that my family was now complete. Within minutes, however, Barry leapt up, saying, 'I must fetch Graeme from your mother; I'm going.' Although this seemed a bit odd at the time, I nevertheless drifted off to sleep. Only later did I understand the pain and agony that Barry must have been wrestling with. He is not a deceitful man, and would have found it painful not to have been honest with me.

At about lunchtime the paediatrician did his rounds in the ward and saw all the mothers whose babies were in his care, except me. As he was walking out of the ward I called to him, 'Dr Judd, you haven't seen me. What about my baby? When can I see him?'

'He's fine,' he replied from the doorway. 'He's in an incubator. I'll see you in the morning.' And he left.

An hour later the gynaecologist was doing his rounds. He stood at my bedside and while checking the wound across my stomach, he asked, 'Are you comfortable?'

'Yes, I'm fine.'

With a kind expression and obvious concern on his face, he said sympathetically, 'Ask the sister in charge if you need anything for pain. I'm really sorry your child has Down syndrome. I didn't do the sterilisation procedure – we never do if there is a problem with the baby. Try and get some sleep and I'll see you tomorrow.' And he too walked away.

I felt disorientated and disembodied – the words 'Down syndrome' kept echoing in my mind, but I couldn't quite take them in. It was clear that the gynaecologist was unaware that I hadn't been told – how is it possible that this was so badly handled? Surely Barry and I should have been told at the same time, when we could draw strength from each other? I firmly believe that the appalling manner in which the news was broken to both of us, had a deleterious effect on our ability to begin understanding and dealing with it. Surely, if what I had been told was true, I couldn't possibly have been sitting there by myself, dazed and afraid – there should have been people explaining things and seeing that I was all right. It was a surreal episode that left me feeling confused.

After a while, an overwhelming feeling of sadness came over me. I slid down in the bed so that the covers hid my face and the tears began rolling uncontrollably down onto my chest. I could not reach for a tissue because my one and only arm was connected to a drip. I felt utterly defeated and unable to put any more effort into life.

I was past caring about anything; the fight had been drained out of me. I was oblivious to everything around me and sobbed quietly to myself. Someone must have noticed my distress, because a nursing sister arrived in a flurry to give me some privacy. She pulled the curtains around my bed, wiped my face with my facecloth and fussed over straightening my bedding. She put her hand on my shoulder and looked at me sympathetically, tears welling up in her eyes.

'I want to see my baby,' I implored, racked by sobs.

'Of course you do,' she said, 'but he's in an incubator and it is just too early for you to be moved. I'll phone the neonatal ward and see how he's doing.'

I lay there trying to imagine what I was going to see when Jonathan was presented to me for the first time. As I lay in the cubicle, alone and disheartened, my thoughts turned to Barry. Where was he? Did he know? Is that why he had dashed off? How was this man, the eternal perfectionist, going to accept this sort of imperfection? More importantly, in retrospect, why was I coping with this alone?

After the first paroxysm of shock had passed, I gingerly started probing at my own emotions. How do I feel about this? Am I strong enough to cope with it? What will coping entail? After a while I felt a calm descending on me like a comfort blanket and I knew, deep within the core of my being, that I would weather this storm and come to terms with the situation. These profound thoughts were interrupted by the sister peeping through a crack in the curtain and saying, 'The staff will be bringing your baby down shortly.'

Now that I was more composed, I was excited, yet apprehensive, about seeing Jonathan for the first time. I heard the sister say, 'Bed number four.' That was me! In the time that it took for the trolley to be pushed across the room, I found myself flooded with powerful and conflicting emotions. My pulse was racing, the blood seemed to rush from my face and I felt a sickening ache in the pit of my stomach. There was a scramble to find the break in the curtain and finally the crib was manoeuvred into the small space between my bed and the window. Because I was immobile, I could not see into the crib from the position that I was in. I didn't know what to expect. Would his appearance be distressing? Would I be able to love this child? The sister came in, still wrestling with the curtain, and leaned over at an awkward angle to lift Jonathan out of the crib. She held him towards me, but realised as she did so that I was not in a position to take him from her with a missing arm on one side and a drip in the other. When she noticed this, she turned him around and placed his head in the crook of my amputated arm, asked if I was all right, and left.

I looked into Jonathan's face for the first time, bracing myself. Of everything I had imagined, the last thing I expected to see was an incredibly beautiful and perfect little boy. I unwrapped the tightly bound blanket to free his arms and legs and as I did so he stirred and briefly looked up at me. I pulled him closer to me so that he could see me and so I could get a closer look at him. As I lifted him towards me, I smelt baby talcum powder and the association of that smell has stayed with me to this day; I will always love it. I examined him from head to toe, and marvelled at his dear little body and beautiful face. Although it was impossible to know what the future would bring, I knew that I would be able to face it with equanimity and love and protect this vulnerable little boy.

When they took him back to the nursery, I felt calm enough to fall into a refreshing and healing sleep.

Teatime was a welcome diversion but I didn't think getting a cup to my mouth could ever be that exhausting. I lay back, breathless from the physical effort involved in sitting up. I was aware of the other mothers in the ward giving me fleeting, nervous glances. At the time I felt hurt, but I now know it was pity and compassion that made them look away. They were celebrating the births of bonny babies and felt guilty because they thought that I wasn't. Looking back now, I felt sorry for those mothers who had so much to celebrate and I was there putting a damper on it. The response of other people, based on what they perceive you to be thinking, has cropped up time and time again since then.

I lay with my eyes closed and was surprised to find myself calmly considering the logistics of where to go from there. How will we cope with telling others who are expecting to hear good news? How will it affect Graeme? And what about Barry? With that I opened my eyes and Barry was standing at the bottom of my bed. He looked pale and drained, and I knew immediately that he must have been aware of Jonathan's condition. I would have liked to have been strong for him and have said something profound and memorable, but instead I burst into tears. He moved around the bed and stood next to me, unsure of how he should respond. Maybe I should have tried to lean forward to embrace him, but I was in a lot of pain, both physically and emotionally. He stood looking at me with tears brimming in his eyes and said, 'We'll have another baby.' This was obviously what he thought I wanted to hear. What better way to make me feel better than to wish Jonathan away? If I had been looking for warning bells, they would have been ringing right then. The comfort for me was more Barry's presence than what he was saying, which didn't really make an impact on me until later. Perhaps he looked so crushed that I chose to overlook what he'd said. He pulled up a chair and I asked him to tell me what had happened while I was under anaesthetic.

Barry was with me for a few hours that Sunday afternoon. He had taken Graeme to my mother so that he could spend time with me. He had not mentioned anything to anyone because he did not know that I was now aware of Jonathan's condition. Barry is not one to broadcast any sort of news in the family, whether it be good or bad.

It was only that afternoon that we decided to call the baby Jonathan. I knew Barry liked the name John, but when I said I preferred Jonathan he agreed, if for no other reason than to placate me. A large part of the afternoon was spent in morose silence. After fussing around me and making sure I was comfortable, Barry went upstairs to the neonatal ward to look at Jonathan through the window, before leaving to pick up Graeme.

It was dinnertime, if five o'clock can ever be called that. My dinner tray stood untouched while the ward was filled with the rattle of cutlery. It had been the first time that day, despite the clatter, that there had been some quiet in the ward. Babies were back in the nursery, sisters and nurses were attending to the handing out of trays, and the mothers had their mouths otherwise occupied. The fact that I was aware of the calm now makes me realise that having people around me at that time must have made me feel vulnerable.

There was quiet time in the ward after dinner, before the visitors arrived. Everyone seemed to have run out of steam by then. Perhaps they knew the routine: the babies would be brought to them in time for the visiting fathers to see them and after that there were disturbed nights with night feeds and nappy changes to look forward to. This lull gave me time to quietly examine my thoughts and I came to the realisation that Jonathan's condition wasn't of catastrophic proportions. I comforted myself with the fact that his appearance was distinctly appealing, and that he was physically well. He was small, but no smaller than any other baby that was born a month premature.

The volatility of my emotions became apparent when, while thinking these consoling thoughts, my mind erupted into panic. Jonathan's birth was not going to be an occasion that would elicit the handing out of cigars or the breaking open of champagne. It is common to deal with the 'here and now' in any situation, but when what you're up against is unknown, it becomes frightening. My concerns at this stage were purely personal. How was I going to tell my mother? What were my friends going to think? How was this child going to fit into a family of achievers? At that moment, my concern was not with Jonathan or me; it was about everyone else in my life. I almost felt as if I should have apologised for bringing this shame into their lives. My thoughts wandered from one irrational idea to the next and suddenly, as if from nowhere, I felt an unexpected and overpowering need to see Jonathan. I wondered where he was and whether the nursing staff were giving him special attention because of his condition. I pictured his little hands and feet and imagined him swathed in his blue blanket with only his head showing, and I know I had a smile on my face.

It felt as though days passed while I was lying there, unable to move, until a staff member came into the ward. She was heading for my bed which I was pleased about because I wanted to ask her when I could see Jonathan. She said, 'Your baby is no longer in the neonatal ward, he's in the nursery. He's doing really well.'

Jonathan had progressed to the nursery and I felt my first surge of pride. I did not know then that I was going to be proud of him his whole life. 'When will I see him?' I asked eagerly. 'The babies will be brought to their mothers a bit later,' she replied.

Some of the mothers in the ward kept their babies in a crib next to them, while others chose to send their babies to the nursery to give them time to rest. The babies of mothers who had had a Caesarean section or a difficult birth and were unable to move comfortably, were kept in the nursery at all times other than for feeds and visits. The mothers were able to visit their babies in the nursery at any time if they were prepared to take the paraphernalia with them, all the pipes and tubes and a drip stand in tow.

It was March and the days were getting shorter; it was already getting dark at around five-thirty. Feeding time was approaching, because there was a cacophony of crying from the nursery. The trolleys started to whizz down the corridor – the louder the squeak, the faster they moved. Through the din I heard familiar footsteps. It was Barry, back for the evening visit. He looked drawn, and had obviously not recovered since I last saw him. The curtains were pulled around the beds to give feeding mothers some privacy and it felt as if we were completely alone. No sooner had Barry arrived than Jonathan was wheeled in, complaining like all the other babies. It was the first time I had heard him cry. The sister on duty popped her head into the cubicle and whispered, 'I'll help you with feeding later.' She obviously thought that either the three of us needed to be alone together for the first time or she might have known that feeding can be a problem for babies with Down syndrome. Jonathan had gone back to sleep and Barry and I just watched him.

'Pick him up,' I said to Barry.

'No, he's asleep,' he replied.

I said again, a bit more firmly, 'Pick him up, Baz!'

Barry looked at me with such pain on his face that I realised for the first time the extent to which he was having difficulty coming to terms with everything that had happened that day. If I'd taken time to think about this or tried to understand it, I probably would've acted differently. But I said impatiently, 'Well, then, pass him to me.'

Barry picked Jonathan up and held him out to me with his

arms extended awkwardly. I could see that he wasn't interested in having a good look at Jonathan. I was very uncomfortable from the surgery and it was not easy for me to get into a comfortable enough position to hold a baby. I had learnt from the previous year that 'where there's a will, there's a way' and the will was certainly there. I wanted to hold Jonathan. With a bit of jiggling around, I found a position in which I could hold him and I looked at Jonathan in a different way. His eyes were open and he looked so much like Graeme that it was uncanny.

I looked up at Barry and said, 'Do you want to hold him?'

'No, it's all right,' he replied, looking uncomfortable.

The writing was on the wall: this was going to be a major obstacle for Barry to overcome and he spent most of the visit looking on in shocked silence. We talked about his day and how Graeme was, as I had been missing him. Barry was due to go on a business trip the following day but he told me how he'd driven into the country to a colleague's home that afternoon to tell him he had decided to cancel the trip in order to be with me.

I unwrapped Jonathan from his blanket and his thin little legs made his nappy look enormous. I examined his stubby fingers and toes and as I looked at him the tears ran down my face. There had been too much disappointment for one day. I wasn't disappointed in him – I was disappointed with how this day had turned out. It was supposed to be the ultimate celebration of new life – a day we had anticipated for a long time and a day that bonded Barry and me together even further, but this did not feel like a celebration.

The bell rang to encourage the visitors to leave and Barry kissed me and put his hand on Jonathan's forehead. It was probably a gesture for my benefit, but it was a gesture nonetheless.

After Barry had gone home I tried to feed Jonathan, which was difficult because he was so lethargic. He was then taken back to the nursery and I spent a few hours, before I went to sleep, going over what had happened that day. It was a day that changed my life forever. I didn't know then that the change would be for the better.

Chapter 3

There's so much I wish I had known the day that Jonathan was born. It would've made it much less painful for me to know that fathers often need time to come to terms with their grief. In the uncertainty of those first few days, it would've been greatly comforting to know that Barry's response to Jonathan was to be expected and normal.

Mothers do not become mothers the day they give birth. They've had life moving around inside them for months before that. The baby is a part of the mother's life long before it's part of the father's. I have heard and read on a few occasions that fathers feel it is an affront to their manhood to produce a child that's less than perfect, but I don't feel that is true. Men are different from women in that they do not have the same emotions and level of sentimentality we do. That's why women are generally the caregivers in families; they feel things at a different emotional level.

At the time of Jonathan's birth, all I really knew was that he had Down syndrome. If he had been genetically normal, I would have known what to expect based on my experience and what is known about children. The only information I had when I looked at him for the first time was that there was something wrong with him. Otherwise he was a stranger to me. I had been given no warning about Jonathan's condition. Some babies with Down syndrome are diagnosed by way of an amniocentesis before birth, but in my case, like in many others, the diagnosis was only made at the time of delivery. There had been no indication up to that point to suggest that anything had gone wrong during my pregnancy.

I have often thought how much gentler it would've been on all of us if, as sometimes happens with other mental disabilities, we had only found out about Jonathan's Down syndrome when he failed to reach milestones. By that time he could have responded to his environment and to us, and enough time would've elapsed since his birth for us to have developed a meaningful relationship with him. Making allowances is so much easier when there is emotional commitment.

It must be extremely difficult for a doctor to have to tell a patient that there is something wrong with their baby. The discomfort on the part of doctors probably contributes to the insensitive way in which it's often handled. 'Do you think your child looks funny?' could certainly have been better expressed.

If Dr Judd had intended only telling me about Jonathan's condition the day after he was born, what motivated him to tell Barry separately? Either he thought Barry would help him with his diagnosis by agreeing that Jonathan looked 'funny' or because emotional sensitivity was not part of the course when he completed his medical degree.

I firmly believe that had the news been broken to Barry and me when we were together, and worded differently, Barry's initial attitude towards Jonathan may have been different. We should have been given the opportunity to draw strength and comfort from each other during that difficult time of uncertainty and sadness.

Over the years, I've come to understand that the doctor's shocking insensitivity regarding his suggestion on institutionalisation of Jonathan may, in fact, have been a strategy. It is true that some new parents are unable to accept that their child has Down syndrome and opt to give the child up. Perhaps Dr Judd was creating the opportunity for us to broach that option.

Only later did I realise that Down syndrome was not my mistake, it was one of nature's blunders. Something went wrong at the time of conception where Jonathan was given one extra chromosome and nature replicated that mistake over and over again into every cell of his body. If I had known that, I would have wrapped my arms around Jonathan on the day he was born to commiserate over the fact that he was the statistic in the Down syndrome risk ratio of 850 to 1. At the time this was the applied factor for women of thirty-three.

The words 'mother' and 'guilt' are synonymous. Mothers always make everything that happens to their children their fault. Although I was perfectly aware that nature should be taking the rap for the gene mutation, I nonetheless blamed myself. Was I at fault for not having him earlier, because I knew that the chances of it happening increased with maternal age? That was an irrational thought, given my circumstances, but I carried on searching for ways to make it my fault. Guilt is such a strong and corrosive emotion, a type of self-administered punishment that has no mercy.

In the months and years that followed Jonathan's birth, I was given beautiful inspirational articles and poems that so often put into words what I was feeling at the time. Emily Perl Kingsley, who has a child of her own with Down syndrome, wrote the following piece that means so much to me called 'Welcome to Holland'. I wish someone had slipped this under my pillow while was I was under the anaesthetic; I could have drawn so much strength from it.

Welcome to Holland

'I am often asked to describe the experience of raising a child with a disability – to try to help people who have not shared that unique experience to understand it, to imagine how it would feel. It's like this . . .

When you're going to have a baby, it's like planning a fabulous vacation trip – to Italy. You buy a bunch of guidebooks and make your wonderful plans. The Colosseum. The Michelangelo David. The gondolas in Venice. You may learn some handy phrases in Italian. It's all very exciting.

After months of eager anticipation, the day finally arrives. You pack your bags and off you go. Several hours later the plane lands. The stewardess comes in and says, "Welcome to Holland."

"Holland?" you say. "What do you mean Holland? I signed

up for Italy! I'm supposed to be in Italy. All my life I've dreamed of going to Italy."

But there's been a change in flight plan. They've landed in Holland and there you must stay.

The important thing is that they haven't taken you to a horrible, disgusting, filthy place, full of pestilence, famine and disease. It's just a different place.

So you must go out and buy new guidebooks. And you must learn a whole new language. And you will meet a whole new group of people who you would never have met.

It's just a different place. It's slower paced than Italy, less flashy than Italy. But after you've been there for a while you catch your breath, you look around, and you begin to notice that Holland has windmills. Holland has tulips. Holland even has Rembrandts.

But everyone you know is busy coming and going from Italy, and they're all bragging about what a wonderful time they had there. And for the rest of your life you will say "Yes, that is where I was supposed to go. That's what I planned."

And the pain of that will never, ever go away, because the loss of that dream is a very significant loss. But if you spend your life mourning the fact that you didn't get to Italy, you may never be free to enjoy the very special, the very lovely, things about Holland.'

If I had known the day that Jonathan was born what I know now, it would not have been a day of turmoil or sadness or checking of his fingers and toes. I would have known that Jonathan was going to light up our lives. Today when I see Graeme and Jonathan together, it is inconceivable that I could ever have wished it to be any different.

Chapter 4

The first day had passed and the worst was over. I have never again questioned why Jonathan was born with Down syndrome or hankered for him to be any different.

One of my mother's favourite quotations is Henry David Thoreau's: 'If a man does not keep pace with his companions, perhaps it is because he hears a different drummer. Let him step to the music which he hears, however measured or far away.' I heard her quoting those words from the time I was a little girl and didn't realise then that they were going to mean so much to me later on in life.

There seemed little point in questioning why Jonathan was number eight hundred and fifty because it wasn't going to change anything. I love the Serenity prayer that talks about 'changing the things you can, accepting the things you can't and knowing the difference'. I acknowledge that the question 'why me' is a symptom of grief and many people need to ask it in order to reach acceptance. One of the first positive steps when faced with the birth of a child with a disability is accepting that it is never going to change. Their condition is not going to go away, no matter how much you would like it to. One is ever hopeful that a mistake has been made in the diagnosis; Barry needed to see the results in black and white before he could consider it a 'fait accompli'.

It was Monday morning and there was the typical early start at the hospital. I'd attempted to feed Jonathan during the night in order to be in sync with everyone else in the ward. He was brought in with all the other babies that morning, which pleased me. I noticed that he was also much better behaved than the other babies who arrived screaming, perhaps because he was always so tired and lethargic. I kept having to remind myself that Jonathan really should still have been growing inside me and was probably not quite ready for the big, wide world. In fact, I was wrong, he was perfectly ready to take on the challenge and the sleepiness and lethargy had nothing to do with being born premature. Newborn babies with Down syndrome can be this way. It makes me chuckle when I think about how, three years later, the only thing that would have kept Jonathan in one place was a straitjacket and a ball and chain!

Because of my arm, I was not able to bath and dress Jonathan at first, but got myself out of bed and watched him being bathed by the nurses for a short while that second day. He was brought back to me spruced up in a yellow babygro and smelling of baby powder. The bath had woken him up and he was more alert than I had previously seen him. He lay next to me on my bed for a long time and I couldn't take my eyes off him. Every time I saw Jonathan, the bond between us became stronger and stronger. A mother's love is supposedly the strongest love of all, but when fierce protection is added to the mix, it makes for a different, all encompassing kind of love.

Barry had popped in to the hospital before work and found me admiring Jonathan. He was still strained and looked as if he'd had little sleep. He said Graeme had gone to nursery school that morning and was very excited about being able to share the news that he had a new brother with the other children. Barry enquired rather unenthusiastically about Jonathan and seemed to want medical facts, rather than anything that resembled emotion. He had contacted Dr Judd, who arranged to meet us in the ward when he did his rounds at ten o'clock. As it was only around eight o'clock, Barry decided to spend some time in the office and be back in time to see Dr Judd. I found out many years later that he had sat in his office that Monday morning with his door closed, his secretary protecting him from seeing anyone or taking any calls. He had been shocked when my arm was amputated, but this was shock of a completely different kind. It is typical of Barry to isolate himself and seek solace from within; he has never been one to look around for someone to lean on in times of trouble.

Barry was back in time for the meeting. Dr Judd greeted us and said, 'I have just examined your son and he looks fine. I believe you know that your son is retarded and I want you to know that you don't have to take him home. You need not see him again.' Even Barry, who at that stage would have loved Jonathan to disappear, looked completely surprised. I was probably more shaken, because Barry had sheltered me from the doctor's first remarks about insti- tutionalising Jonathan. Feeling stunned, it took me a minute before I could indignantly retort, 'His name is Jonathan and we're taking him home.' Barry was not given any choice – I had made the decision. Perhaps it was not fair at the time, but it was an instinctive and automatic response.

'These children often present problems in the home,' Dr Judd added. This was when, having been advised in no uncertain terms that Jonathan was coming home with us, he should have begun offering us practical advice and supplying us with relevant information. What a shame that he had no true understanding of the enormity of our situation. Many people consider a doctor's opinion sacrosanct, and he is therefore placed in a uniquely powerful position, in that he is able to positively or negatively influence them. How different things might have been for us if Dr Judd had provided positive support and reinforcement.

When he finally realised that Jonathan was cherished in the same way as all the other babies in the nursery, he was able to talk to us about him in the same way he would have discussed any other baby with any other parents. I think it broke the tension once he knew what our intentions were or, more accurately, what my intentions were. Although I didn't like his attitude or manner, I respected him as a good diagnostician and recognised that some of my negative feelings towards him were probably related to 'shooting the messenger'.

Barry dragged a chair across the ward and sat down heavily next to my bed. Either the bed was very high or the chair was unusually low, because I remember looking down at Barry, almost from a disembodied height, sitting with his shoulders hunched and his head in his hands. The past forty-eight hours had passed by in a blur, and this was the first time I realised the extent of the pain and confusion he was feeling. Tears welled up in my eyes as I registered this pathetic sight; I had up until now regarded his unhappy demeanour as disappointment that would soon pass, rather than a soul-searing inability to come to terms with Jonathan's condition. In that fleeting moment, I dimly perceived that it could mean serious trouble for the future of our family.

Soon it was feeding time and Jonathan's crib was rolled in. A young paediatric nurse lifted Jonathan out of his crib and handed him to Barry. This time he wasn't so quick to pass him on to me like he was playing 'pass the parcel'. He looked at him and said, in a bewildered tone, 'But he's so like Graeme.'

'Yes,' I said, not wanting to close the door on comparison. 'Look at his hands and feet, they're so cute. Just like Graeme's were.'

This was actually far from true. Jonathan had typical Down syndrome feet and hands with short stubby fingers and toes and wide hands and feet, with the characteristic curved baby finger and gap between his big and second toe. Barry put Jonathan into my arms and said he needed to get back to work. It was clear that he was still in shock and couldn't associate the fact that Jonathan, who was deemed to be 'damaged', was as beautiful and well formed as his genetically normal brother.

I had asked Barry to phone my mother and tell her that Jonathan had Down syndrome. There was a stunned silence as she absorbed what Barry was saying. He asked her to let the rest of the family know and I presume that that was how my family heard about Jonathan.

Lunchtime was over, the babies were back in the nursery, and I was resting. My mind was relatively calm, but if I had known that Barry was alone in his office, desperately trying to deal with his grief, it would not have been. Then, as if from nowhere, my mother and eldest sister Cathy were standing at the foot of my bed. They were laden with flowers and gifts. Cath's eyes were red and swollen from crying, and that gave me licence to show some emotions of my own. My mom, looking uncharacteristically ill at ease and flustered, said, 'Are you sure they haven't made a mistake? Perhaps they're wrong. Doctors can make mistakes.'

The test that confirms the chromosomal abnormality of Down syndrome took six weeks to process in those days. So we had to accept that Jonathan did have Down syndrome until the results showed otherwise. They had taken a sample of blood from him just after his birth for the test.

Cath hadn't been there long when she said, 'I want to see Jonathan. Do you think they will let me look at him through the nursery window?' She dashed off to speak to the staff and came back to take Mom with her. Jonathan was apparently in his yellow babygro and Cath still talks about how tiny he was then when she stands next to him now. When I asked her to describe her feelings she said, 'With my very first glimpse of him, I felt such an overpowering surge of love that I burst into tears. He was so fragile and perfect looking and I loved him instantly and completely.' You might think that these words were engineered to fit a touching story. On the contrary, these words have been acted out over sixteen years. She has been a devoted aunt to Jonathan and a very worthy godmother.

I had been dreading interacting with other people, possibly because everyone in the hospital had been tiptoeing around me or approaching me with caution and handling me with kid gloves. My mother has a way of showing her sadness, but always portrays strength, probably from having to do so many times in her own life. It was a huge relief to find that I could be myself and let my guard down while my family was there. There's nothing more reassuring than family at a time of crisis and while I had brothers and sisters living in other countries, and there was the distance between us, I still felt connected to them. I think it can be called 'pooling resources', the gathering of everything dear and meaningful in your life to see you through crises. I had thought about my father the night before and instead of feeling sad, I felt content in the belief that he would have accepted Jonathan just as I did and loved him for being my son. He was a man with a great capacity to care and it is tragic that he never had the opportunity to love and care for his grandchildren.

Mom and Cath didn't stay long. They could see I was tired and the ward sister had said that they were coming to take down my drip and remove the catheter. With that came a welcome freedom. It takes losing the use of both hands to appreciate the use of one! A little while later my friend Margie arrived. Margie and I had worked together before either of us were married. She looked pale and out of breath. She had probably run up the stairs to get to me in a hurry. It was typical of Margie to be where the trouble was – she had never been a coward when it came to responding to other people's tragedies. She handed me a card and in the envelope was a little notebook that she had written in. It was filled with quotations on life's joys and was as precious to me then as it is to me now. She must have spent the morning writing them down, as she had only heard about Jonathan earlier that morning when she phoned Barry. One of the quotes she had chosen was 'The finest gifts we get are from those who have nothing but themselves to give'. She may not have intended to refer to herself, but it was appropriate that it came from someone who gave of herself so willingly. Margie and her family have been an integral part of Jonathan's life since then and I know they always will be.

By the time Margie had left it was time for feeding and, like everyone else in the ward, I was excited to hear the noise of the trolleys being pushed around. Feeding Jonathan did not get any easier and I had resorted to attempting to get glucose down his throat in a feeding bottle. People with Down syndrome tend to have smaller than average mouths and bigger than usual tongues. It was easier for him to have food dripped down his throat with the occasional squeeze of the bottle when the dripping seemed too slow or I became impatient. He was totally disinterested in food and had trouble staying awake, while I anxiously tried to encourage him to eat.

During visiting time that evening Barry brought Graeme with him. Children were not allowed in the ward, but because I was no longer attached to a catheter and drip, I was able to walk to the visitors' area to be with him. Graeme was very excited about seeing his new brother, so before we sat down we went to the nursery window to see Jonathan. Graeme was not aware that there was anything wrong with him. If we had been able to find the right words to tell him that his brother was not genetically normal, I think he would have reacted in the same way he did that night. It would have made no difference then and it makes no difference now. Graeme has a special nature that, from the outset, allowed him to accept Jonathan unconditionally. I have so many treasured memories of them playing together and Graeme responding to Jonathan at his level of understanding. From the beginning, Graeme exhibited an intuitive love and protection for Jonathan that was inexplicable in a child of his age.

While we were at the window admiring Jonathan lying in his crib, which had been pushed forward for us to see into, Barry picked Graeme up so that he could get a better view. Barry had a tremulous smile on his face when he saw Graeme's contagious excitement. Graeme's eyes lit up and he started waving frantically at Jonathan, just as a three-year-old does when he wants to say hello. I happened to glance at Barry's face at that moment, and my knees went weak with relief at what I saw. He was looking at Jonathan, obviously caught up in the moment and responding to Graeme's enthusiasm, with an expression of pride, something I hadn't seen until then. This small gesture was very welcome, but there would still be a long road to travel before things got better.

Chapter 5

The next few days came and went with me feeling a little bit stronger every day and Jonathan getting the idea that a feeding bottle was going to be pushed into his mouth at fairly regular intervals. His attitude towards it seemed to be one of indifference. If I was going to insist on getting food down him, he was going to lie there and allow it. He didn't fight for it, nor did he object.

Each time this little boy was brought to me for feeding I loved him more and more. It was no longer just a feeling of protection, I was now besotted with him. His slow, lethargic movements exuded a calm that made me feel at ease. I had hardly heard him cry, which was in stark comparison to the other babies in the ward who arrived screaming for food.

Because the response of parents to the birth of a baby with Down syndrome differs, there is obvious confusion about how to treat the situation. It sticks out in my mind how, when people approached me while I was still in hospital, they seemed to be searching for clues as to how I felt. They looked at my face for cues and hesitated before they said anything; that is a standard response and a wise one. What a mistake it would be to fly into the hospital ward and say to a new mother, 'God, I'm so sorry, you must be so disappointed!', when she is just coming to terms with that disappointment. All parents will know that they can show disappointment in their children, but nobody else must suggest it. It was a reminder to me in those first few days of how different people are when it comes to dealing with emotional issues. Some people can't, some people battle but try, and for some it just happens naturally. I suppose it depends on what sort of relationship you have had with people in the past. Family and friends visited me and it was pretty clear that some could not find words to express their support for this confusing mix of sadness and congratulations. How would they know how to respond when they didn't know how I was feeling?

I was sent beautiful flowers, and family and friends arrived with thoughtful and generous gifts for Jonathan. I have kept the cards that were attached to the gifts and have enjoyed looking at them from time to time. The ones that said the right thing for me were the ones that said, 'We know he is going to bring you a lot of joy.' Those words made no apology for Jonathan not being genetically normal and did not suggest disappointment. They were also very true words. Although that is what I wanted to hear, I know a few people who have been in the same situation who thought it insensitive to mention the future when they were having so much trouble dealing with the present. I heard one parent say, 'I didn't want anyone near me who was going to tell me how lucky I was or how I'd been specially chosen. These people normally hand out printed poems containing syrupy platitudes.' I think she could only admit feeling like that because she had turned out to be one of the most dedicated parents. We all have our own ways of coping, none of them right or wrong.

My sister Pat gave me a booklet of handwritten coupons, each one stating, 'This coupon can be exchanged for a session of babysitting, any time of the day or night and is valid for life'. In small print at the bottom it said, 'Nappy changes not included'. It raised a smile, but also had a message for me that said 'I'm here and always will be'.

I remember a few years later, during a meeting, one of the mothers at the nursery school said, 'I balk at the sentimentality connected to children with Down syndrome. If that time and effort was spent more constructively, our children would benefit from it.'

There seems to be a system that operates in disability circles. Articles and poems that inspire and console seem to reach every corner. I have asked many parents if they have seen a particular article and they always have. Some object to the sentimentality, but I have drawn comfort from them, as have most mothers I know.

Barry had been popping in to see me at odd times during the day. In the evenings he'd bring Graeme with him and we would all stand and admire Jonathan through the glass and comment on his every twitch. I could see that Barry had still not come to terms with the situation. I asked him to bring his camera that afternoon so we could take some photographs of Jonathan to send to Margaret, my sister in Australia. I took a picture of Barry holding Jonathan and it certainly was not a typical happy snap for the family album. His unhappiness hurt me deeply. I'd seen both doctors that day and they had decided that I could go home with Jonathan the following day.

Tomorrow was the day, the start of a whole new life and we would not have to look at Jonathan through glass anymore. While we were standing there one evening, Graeme got a worried look on his face and asked, 'Do you think I would drop Jonathan if I had to hold him?' and I replied, 'Not if you don't open your arms.' Even Barry laughed. I was looking forward to leaving the hospital, it was time to get on with our lives whatever the challenges were. Although I loved Jonathan very much, I was still very afraid of what lay ahead. If I had known then the words of Bil Keane, a hugely popular American comic writer, I would probably have savoured the moment and let tomorrow take care of itself. They read, 'Yesterday's the past, tomorrow's the future, but today is a gift. That's why it is called the present.'

Chapter 6

The next day dawned and I was allowed to go home after both doctors had seen me. The ward staff promised to phone Barry when I was ready to be collected. I bathed Jonathan for the first time that morning. I think the staff wanted to make sure I was capable of bathing my floppy rag doll baby with one hand. I passed the test and the special little white outfit was ready and waiting for the big event. Jonathan was wrapped in a towel after his bath and I unwrapped him and put him on the bed to dress him. I put a disposable nappy and a vest on, and then reached out to pick up the white suit and as I lifted his legs to start dressing him, I saw that he had a dirty nappy. It's a regular occurrence with newborn babies that you have no sooner changed them than they need another nappy. I opened his nappy and saw, to my horror, that it was filled with blood. As I scooped him up into my arms I noticed he was blue. I ran with him down the hospital corridor, shouting for help. A sister heard me and grabbed him out of my arms and rushed to the oxygen dispenser on the wall. She pulled the mask down, but could not get the oxygen to flow. That unit was not working, so she ran with him up the stairs, along the passage and into the neonatal ward. This meant going up a staircase to another floor and along a long corridor – an interminable amount of time for a child who was not breathing. I was behind her, unable to keep up because I still had stitches in my stomach. I went into the neonatal ward and was asked to wait in the parents' waiting room down the hall while they attended to Jonathan. I stood outside the door, unable to move. Jonathan's blood was on my dressing gown and I knew this was serious. Eventually a doctor came to speak to me and said Dr Judd would be called, but that there was a paediatric surgeon on hand, who could give an opinion. The best thing would be for me to wait in the ward and they would see me when they had a better idea of what the problem was.

I went back to the ward and found Barry waiting, unaware that anything was wrong. One of the sisters had phoned him to say I was ready to go home and he had come to fetch us. It must have been evident as I walked into the ward, that something was very wrong. He leapt up from the chair and came towards me. 'What's wrong?' he said.

I could not find the words to tell him. I was not able to think about what had just happened, let alone talk about it. I gazed at Barry and said, 'The doctor will come and talk to us.'

He looked down at the blood on my dressing gown and said, 'Are you all right?' How I wished it was me that had the problem.

'I'm fine,' I replied. I sat on the side of my bed next to the little white piece of baby clothing and stared out of the window, numb with fear. Barry held my hand, waiting for me to tell him what was going on. I gathered myself and said, 'He's sick, Jonathan is sick.'

'What do you mean sick?' he said.

'He had blood in his nappy,' and as I said it, it sounded trivial, as if I was overreacting.

'What did the doctor say?' he said.

'I haven't seen him yet. They told me in the neonatal ward that they would ask Dr Judd to come down and see us once he's examined Jonathan.'

'The neonatal ward?' Barry said. 'What is he doing there?'

I snapped at him: 'I told you, he's sick!'

We sat there for about an hour, although it felt more like a day. Finally Dr Judd came flying into the ward, his white coat flapping behind him. 'I need to talk to you both,' he said. 'Your son is ill and I have called in a surgeon to have a look at him.'

'A surgeon?' Barry exclaimed.

'Yes,' he said. 'He has NEC and this condition comes with a very high mortality rate. I think because of his Down syndrome, your son stands very little chance of survival.' He explained that NEC was a condition where the bowel threatens to perforate. NEC stands for necrotising enterocolitis, a condition that occurs in some premature babies. I have never heard of another baby with Down syndrome having it. That was Jonathan; unlucky to have Down syndrome and now unlucky to have NEC. The surgeon needed to be on call at all times in case the bowel perforated.

I later found out that two other babies, both boys, were in the neonatal ward at the same time with the same condition. I have often wondered about that. It seems strange that three babies, all delivered by Caesarean section had NEC – was it contagious? I have also wondered over the years whether the defective oxygen machine caused Jonathan to have further brain damage, given the fact that he had to be rushed to another floor and was very blue by the time he got there. Although these thoughts have entered my head, there seems little point in pursuing them. What good would it do? Once again the prayer comes up about learning to accept the things that you can't change.

I didn't notice at the time, but later I realised that Dr Judd could not bring himself to use Jonathan's name. The thought probably occurred to me because Jonathan was so important in my life and it was clear that he was merely a medical case to the doctor. I don't suppose we should expect doctors to attach any emotions to their cases, or they would not be able to do their work. It would just not work if a paediatrician had to dab his eyes when he told you your child was sick.

Dr Judd started explaining that Jonathan's bowel needed to be rested and he would be fed intravenously for ten days. Nothing could go down his throat. I don't think it worried Jonathan too much because he never seemed too enamoured of the idea of eating anyway. Dr Judd said we should give them a chance in the neonatal ward to set up all the equipment and we could then go up and see him. Promising to keep us informed about Jonathan's progress, Dr Judd left in the same flurry as he arrived.

Barry pulled the curtain between my bed and the next. He

sat down on the chair and buried his head in his hands. It is never pleasant to see a grown man cry, but even less when he stands six foot four inches tall and normally looks absolutely impenetrable. He looked up at me, his face contorted with pain, and said, 'I don't want him to die.' That was enough for me to lose all control and the floodgates opened. This was such a different pain to the one we had felt five days before, and it was clear that Jonathan's birth had not brought pain, but fear had. Fear of the unknown. Now we had something we knew: Jonathan might die.

We waited and waited to be called to the neonatal ward. Sick with worry, we decided to go upstairs and look through the glass window into the ward in the hope of finding a clue that everything was going to be all right. It had struck me as I sat on my bed downstairs that Dr Judd had misjudged what my attitude would be towards Down syndrome, and perhaps he was misjudging this situation too. Perhaps Jonathan was going to be fine. It also struck me at that time that I wasn't supposed to have had children, if the doctors were to be believed. I think it was those thoughts that jostled me up the stairs. Perhaps Barry's tight grip on my hand also helped.

We stood there trying to spot Jonathan. There was another couple standing next to us, also grey with anxiety and probably also hoping that a staff member would pop out of the ward and say, 'The crisis is over, he's going to be fine.' We stood at that window often during the next few weeks with other parents and grandparents. That space between the back wall and the glass window is a place, reserved in the world, where what you do, where you come from or how well adjusted you are, is totally irrelevant. When you stand there you are only a parent. The people you stand with are only parents. You are stripped of your past and your future. The only ambition you have while you stand there is to continue being a parent.

We could not make sense of what was going on. There were about eight incubators with babies in them and four cribs. We couldn't see into the cribs, other than a blue or pink blanket, which was the only clue in our search for Jonathan. All the babies in the incubators were only wearing nappies, which made them look alike and the incubators were not all facing the same way, so it was hard to see into some of them. There was a lot of staff activity too. A few incubators had nurses' or doctors' hands pushed into them. We were traumatised by what we were looking at. The best of all the options, if we had to choose any, was probably to find Jonathan wrapped in a blue blanket in a portable crib.

We still hadn't spotted Jonathan and Barry was becoming impatient. In this situation mothers are prepared to wait as long as it takes if they feel that the waiting will make the situation better. Barry, in keeping with his inability to accept that there is such a colour as grey, wanted to know the facts. Without saying anything, he dashed off and I watched from the glass window as he quizzed a staff member. He beckoned me to join him.

The sister in charge of the unit came to meet us and was very warm and friendly. She explained that we would be able to come in to see our child, but that there were strict rules in place for parents who entered the unit. We had to wash our hands with a red, putrid smelling liquid and put on a gown before we entered. She pointed us in the direction of the basins and gowns, which were individually wrapped in sterile parcels. While we got ready I wondered how long we would have waited there or in the ward to get the opportunity to be with Jonathan. We were led to an incubator that we would not have been able to see from the viewing window. There was Jonathan, lying on his stomach, his head turned to one side with tubes everywhere. The memory of that first sight of Jonathan in the incubator still makes me nauseous. Only a parent who has had to watch a very sick child can relate to the agony. Barry put his arm around my shoulders, waiting for my response. I continued to stare at Jonathan, trying to absorb the horrific sight, the tears rolling down my face. All my hopes about the doctors being wrong were dashed. He was clearly a very sick child.

Guilt is a powerful and destructive emotion. It attacks what's in the heart and disregards what's in the head. No amount of logic could have convinced me that this was not my fault. Why did I cry when I heard he had Down syndrome? This was my punishment. As I stood there unable to utter a sound, I promised myself that if Jonathan recovered, I would never again question why he was different, but rejoice that he was alive. If I was feeling tormented, I was sure Barry was feeling worse. There were no words to comfort each other, so we stood there in desperate despair.

Above left: *Graeme holds Jonathan for the first time.*
Above right: *Jonathan as a toddler.*
Below: *The bond between Jonathan and Graeme developed at a very young age.*

Top left: *Barry and Jonathan.*
Top right: *Jonathan was not able to hold his head up until he was 9 months old.*
Above: *Barry's first real connection with Jonathan.*

Jonathan growing up.

Above left: *The cot Jonathan slept in until he was four years old.*

Above right: *Milly at the Sunshine Centre reading to Jonathan.*

Right: *Jonathan's first day at Sunfield.*

Above: *A concert at Golden Hours.*
Below: *Jonathan's eighth birthday.*

Left: *A recent picture of Liz and Jonathan.*
Below: *Jonathan and Graeme complete a trial swim at Sun City.*

Opposite top & left:
The relationship between Graeme and Jonathan is a very close and special one.
Opposite right: *The night of Jonathan's dance.*

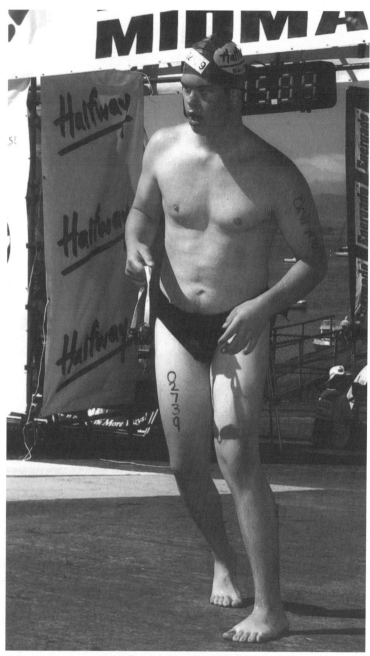

A proud Jonathan finishes the 2003 Midmar Mile.
(Photograph courtesy of Portrait Place)

Chapter 7

The neonatal ward felt like a different world; vulnerable, temporary and connected to reality only by a thread. The staff had been trained to acknowledge and respect the parents' pain and their right to be with their child. It was very difficult to spend long periods there, because parents had no real function or role to play. The very ill babies did not get fed per mouth and were unable to be moved from their incubators because of the drips, tubes and pipes attached to them. Parents could only stand watching, hoping, praying and feeling that they were very much in the way. It felt as if Jonathan was no longer our business and we were very lucky to be there at all. That perhaps does not describe the feeling of isolation too well, because it makes it sound as if the staff had something to do with it. The feeling is better described as absolute helplessness. You stand and watch your child fight to survive and there is nothing you can do to make a difference. I think it burns a hole in a mother's heart that never heals. Every time Jonathan has been sick since then, the thought of him in that incubator haunts me. All parents worry about their children getting sick, but those who have experienced it have something very frightening to base their fears on. It appears to be human nature to believe that bad things can only happen to others.

I'm sure all parents who have had a really sick child feel a lot more vulnerable and a lot less exempt from illness, because they have the pictures in their minds and the burn holes in their hearts.

The only clues we have, as parents, of how happy or healthy our babies are is how well they are eating, sleeping, crying and putting on weight. Jonathan was doing none of these things, other than sleeping. I had only the doctor's words to go on and they echoed in my head over and over again: 'Very little chance of survival.' We stayed in the neonatal ward for about an hour, both becoming more and more distressed, and feeling more and more helpless as we watched Jonathan's almost lifeless body. I recognised that I needed to sit or lie down and Barry took me back to my ward, where I collapsed in a heap from the physical and mental strain – it had only been five days since Jonathan's birth. I looked at Barry sitting next to me on the chair that had supported him through so much anguish, and he once again looked crushed. The dark rings under his eyes were testimony to the strain of the last five days.

Barry stayed with me for the day and we went up to the neonatal ward several times. Each time we felt the same hopelessness but remained driven by the thought that tomorrow might bring new hope. If I had been spared that day, I would have been at home starting my new life that included Jonathan. But would that new life have had as much value, if I didn't have this day to compare it with? I have always known that things happen for a reason and I knew the purpose of this was not to teach me to be more charitable, a thought I tormented myself with, but to show me to look for beauty in the most unlikely places. I would have taken

Jonathan home that day feeling slightly cheated and uncertain about the future. How different it was when we finally did take him home. We had been put to the test, and we really did want Jonathan in our lives.

Tomorrow arrived and there was still no change in Jonathan's condition. It was decided that I would go home and travel between home and the hospital to be with Jonathan. Graeme was only three and he must have been getting some clear messages that things were not going according to plan. Having a second child always changes a parent's relationship with the first, no matter how hard you try to avoid it or deny it. Very often the change in the relationship is beneficial, as it creates the opportunity for the older child to develop and grow emotionally. I have often noticed how firstborn children have a certain strength and fortitude. I was pleased to be going home to spend time with Graeme.

Leaving the hospital was surprisingly traumatic. I was going to be spending four or five hours a day with Jonathan, but going home without a baby upset me. My life was filled with heart machines and drip alarms, and home seemed so quiet in comparison. Graeme was thrilled to see me and showed it in the enthusiastic way I have always loved about him. We had tea before Barry went back to the office and I explained to Graeme that his brother was not well, but that we would take him to see him when Dad got home from work. Graeme was not well either; he had had a cold for a few days and I noticed that he had a fever and was complaining of a sore ear. I phoned the doctor to make an appointment for later that day, after I had been to the hospital to see Jonathan.

It was strange to be in the neonatal ward as a non-patient, fully dressed instead of in bedclothes and in contact with the outside world. As I parked the car and battled out of the seat, holding on to my stitched-up stomach, I imagined myself getting to Jonathan's incubator to find him awake and looking around. But I felt a sense of disappointment when I got there as there was no change. The surgeon was there and explained to me that he was checking on him a few times a day and was 'on call' at all times. He reminded me that Jonathan was desperately ill, but was doing well under the circumstances. It takes situations like this to appreciate the advances that have been made in medical science. I stayed with Jonathan for a couple of hours and watched, in horror, as the doctor changed the drip to another vein. Although it was nerve-racking, I felt the greatest respect for his ability to work on the tiniest of veins.

When Jonathan was settled after the ordeal, I went home to fetch Graeme to take him to our family doctor. He was surprised to see me so soon, as he had heard of Jonathan's birth. As I arrived in his examining room, he said, 'You must still have stitches, what are you doing here?' I explained that Graeme wasn't well and Jonathan was still in hospital. He remarked on how resilient I was, examined Graeme and gave him an antibiotic for an ear infection. I got home and was settling down to find some quiet time to return a few phone calls, when someone called Gail from the Down Syndrome Association phoned. She had been informed by the hospital of Jonathan's birth and wanted to come and meet us and answer any questions we might have. She made arrangements to come to our home that evening after we had been to visit Jonathan. Although we had promised to take Graeme to the hospital with us, we were concerned about him not being well and possibly taking infection into the hospital. Graeme was disappointed, but I was relieved not to have to explain to him what had happened and to see his face when he saw his brother in an incubator with multiple attachments. It had been a long day and that could wait for tomorrow.

Barry and I stood next to the incubator; I had been holding Jonathan's little hand through the hole for half an hour, and when I let go, Barry reached in. It was such a contrast, those minute fingers resting in his giant hand. Was it a hand he was holding out to Jonathan or was it an olive branch? I recognised that it may have been the latter, despite the pain and worry that usually made me insensitive to anything else while I was standing next to the incubator. This was the first sign of voluntary interaction between Barry and Jonathan and although there was no reason to feel better about Jonathan's state of health, I left the neonatal ward that night feeling better than when I arrived.

Gail arrived at eight o'clock that evening, as arranged. It must be very hard for a person to counsel couples who are strangers and whose reaction to the Down syndrome birth is unknown. She looked very apprehensive and it made me realise what dedicated work she was doing. This was a voluntary undertaking on her part and her only reward was the knowledge that she was able to assist people in our position, particularly because she had had a baby with Down syndrome seven years earlier. We must have been a very difficult couple to counsel, because we wanted to know everything. Barry needs to know all the facts before he can accept anything. He cut to the chase in the first few sentences by asking, 'How long is he going to live?' Gail did not look as shocked as I must have and replied, 'Barry, people with Down syndrome today have a much higher chance of living a long and healthy life because of the developments made in medicine. With antibiotics and advanced heart surgery, there is no reason why people with Down syndrome should not live to be fifty.' Shuffling in his chair, Barry seemed to be getting more comfortable, possibly because he liked what he was hearing. He continued this line of questioning, 'How retarded will he be?' Gail kept very cool and said, 'People with Down syndrome vary in their potential. Their ability varies in just the same way as genetically normal people. Some of us are brighter and have more potential than others and some of us have more opportunities in which to develop and grow.' We both liked that one too. I think we were both thinking that this was going to be the first Down syndrome Einstein.

Before I met Barry and between my overseas trips, I was a volunteer at the Avril Elizabeth Home, a large care centre for mentally disabled children. It was home for many young children. I worked there every Sunday for a few years and was always attracted to the children with Down syndrome, so much so that I got permission a few times to take two of the boys home with me for lunch. One of the boys was called Martin and he was about six years old at the time. Because of the characteristic speech difficulty people with Down syndrome have, he could not say 'Liz' properly and called me 'Lik'. This was a source of great amusement to my younger brother Pete, who was a teenager at the time. He continued to call me Lik and the name stuck. Barry still calls me 'Lik' in private and when he teases me and the irony always hits really hard when Jonathan calls me 'Mommy Lik'. It was during that time that I first made it my business to find out about Down syndrome, so some of what Gail was telling us I already knew.

Gail gave us all the facts we wanted and seemed to have all the statistics at her fingertips. She left literature for us to read and a telephone number where she could be contacted at any time. Although Gail was not the purveyor of good news or of wonderful times ahead, we felt comforted in knowing the facts, good and not so good. We didn't want any more surprises; if there was bad news, we wanted to know it there and then.

Chapter 8

Visits to the ward continued four times a day, as well as regular consultations with the doctors over Jonathan's prognosis. There seemed to be no progress; he was no better or worse. One often becomes used to seeing someone sick and in conditions that originally shocked one, but I was traumatised each time I saw him. It was the weekend and we had spent more time than usual with Jonathan that Sunday, because the staff had told us he had been restless in the early hours. It was also easier, being the weekend, because Graeme could stay with my mother. She was always protective of him and felt that he didn't need to see what was going on.

While we were in the ward at around noon, we noticed that Jonathan seemed uncomfortable and distressed. We alerted the staff and both the paediatrician and surgeon arrived soon thereafter, and we were asked to step outside the ward while they examined him. We went to the viewing window, the place reserved for anxious parents. We could not see what was going on, but felt that we were on hand if they needed us. The last eight days had shown us what the drill was when something went wrong, but seeing Jonathan in obvious discomfort confirmed that our worry was justified.

His condition had deteriorated and was now ranked as critical. There was a debate between the doctors as to whether it was the right time to operate on him or not. Jonathan looked weak and delicate and I was relieved when the surgeon told us that they were going to see what the next twenty-four hours brought, before they made any decisions. Nursing was stepped up and there was someone at Jonathan's side at all times. He must have been given medication in his drip to calm him, because he had fallen asleep. We remained in the ward for the rest of the day, too scared and distraught to move.

At four o'clock a group of people gathered around another incubator in the ward. I wasn't sure why so many people were there, but soon realised that it was a baptism for a very sick baby. We were standing with Jonathan, searching for any signs of improvement and I think the idea occurred to both of us at the same time. As the minister was about to leave the ward, Barry walked over to talk to him. 'I also have a very sick baby, would you please baptise him?' He was clearly honoured by the request and asked no questions about who we were or what faith we practised. He baptised Jonathan and although Jonathan had an official baptism with all the family present once he was well, I will always consider that to be his christening. I stood looking on, desperately sad and afraid, hoping Jonathan was not going to treat this as a reason to give up fighting for his life.

The weekend was almost over and we fetched Graeme from my mom. We had decided to tell him about Jonathan's condition as he'd asked about going to the hospital every time we spoke to him on the phone that weekend. Barry and I discussed it in the car on the way to fetch him and decided to take him with us to the hospital that evening. It was cold and I remember that Graeme was wearing a jacket that had a hood with fur around the edge which framed his face. Before we left for the hospital we explained to Graeme that Jonathan was not in the same place he had seen him before and that he needed medicine because he wasn't feeling very well. Graeme seemed to accept that and jumped around excitedly in anticipation.

We got to the neonatal ward and I went inside while Graeme and Barry stood at the viewing window. I looked at Jonathan and it was as if he hadn't moved at all since I had last seen him. I glanced over at the window. Barry had picked Graeme up and was holding him on his hip. The incubator had been moved closer to the viewing window, so they could see Jonathan fairly clearly. I caught a glimpse of Graeme's face through the glass and his expression will always be etched in my memory, along with so many other things. Graeme has always had a happy face and expressive eyes and that night he had bright red cheeks and looked like an Eskimo, with his furry hood. When I caught sight of him, he had just spotted Jonathan. That look has appeared on Graeme's face only a few times in his life, and the next time I saw it was when Jonathan was seriously ill again. There is no description for it other than despair. I stood there, my heart breaking. One child was seriously ill, and the other seriously traumatised. The only thing Graeme uttered was, 'Why can't Jonathan be with the other babies?' I would also have loved Jonathan to have been downstairs where Graeme had seen him last. Barry then spent some time with Jonathan and I held Graeme at the window, viewing this sad place from a different perspective. The incubator of the baby who had been baptised that afternoon was empty, which was deeply disturbing.

While Barry was in the neonatal ward with Jonathan, the sister in charge of the unit told him that the doctor had left a message saying that Jonathan's condition had stabilised and they didn't think surgery was a consideration at that time. Although Graeme's distress had been upsetting, we all went home feeling considerably more hopeful and with our spirits slightly lifted. Every night since Jonathan had become ill, I had lain awake trying to make sense of it all. It was difficult, no matter how hard I tried, to imagine Jonathan well. We had seen him sick for as long as we'd seen him well – would he just wake up and start looking around or would he start shouting to be fed? There were so many questions nobody could answer, the most important being, if the bowel was going to perforate, why had it not done so in the past four days and at what point would we know that it was no longer a threat? Obviously these questions were hard to answer and I had to be happy with the non-committal replies I was getting from the doctors.

Nothing much changed until Tuesday. By then ten days had passed and that concluded the rest period the doctors had prescribed for Jonathan's bowel. When I got there that morning, one of the sisters rushed past me in the doorway and shouted, 'Your little man is going to have something to eat today.' Needless to say, I was thrilled at this development, but couldn't imagine how they were going to get him to take food, because I had battled even when he was well. When the same sister stopped at Jonathan's incubator to take his temperature about ten minutes later, I asked how they were going to manage this and she replied, 'Hang around and you'll see.' It takes a special kind of person to do this work while remaining cheerful and competent, never showing any signs of panic or uncertainty. Medical personnel like this are worth their weight in gold, as their positive attitude is contagious and comforting for worried parents. There were a few extremely sick babies in the neonatal ward, not only the ones that were there temporarily after their birth. I was nervous and excited – this promised to be a momentous day.

Once the sister had written up the charts of some of the other babies, she headed towards Jonathan, saying, 'Right, little man, it's your turn.' She raised the lid of the incubator and carefully untangled all the tubes and pipes. She then lifted him up, deftly holding onto all the paraphernalia at the same time, and moved him onto a big changing counter. It was remarkable to see the confidence and expertise with which she handled him, making it look so easy. She then brought over all she needed to start the feeding process. I was a little confused because I thought it would include a feeding bottle, but she had a syringe, a tube and a measure of feeding formula. Chatting cheerfully to Jonathan while she worked, she changed his nappy, then announced, 'It's breakfast time!' and started pushing the thin tube up his nose. He coughed and spluttered, but the tube continued down his nasal passage. When she was happy that it was in place, she poured a measured amount of formula, using the syringe, down the tube into his stomach. He lay there as if nothing had happened. That was breakfast and he hadn't even noticed he'd had it. He was going to be tube fed for some time, which presented a problem because he was not learning to suck. The sister turned to me and said, 'Pull over that chair and sit down.' I did so and she gently put him in my arms, arranging the pipes around him. It felt like a really special occasion to be holding Jonathan again. He was so delicate and I thought I would be frightened, but it felt so comfortable and natural. I have heard that mothers whose babies are sick just after their birth, are often unable to bond with them because of the lack of contact. I can understand how that can happen, particularly with a baby who looks so small and helpless. I was lucky that Jonathan had been well for the first four days of his life and I had securely bonded with him then, even if it was initially with shock and uncertainty regarding his Down syndrome.

I held him for about an hour and although I didn't have that much to be relieved about, because nothing much had changed, it was good to have him in my arms. I had often wondered if I would ever hold him again. He fell asleep with a full stomach and the sister returned and helped with the tubes while I put him back in the incubator. I went down to the hospital cafeteria to have a cup of tea with a friend, but went back to check that he'd kept the food down before leaving the hospital.

I spent the day toing and froing between home, the hospital and Graeme's nursery school, and the next few days were much the same. Jonathan was tube fed three times a day and I held him after every feed. Barry, Graeme and I then went back to the hospital in the evenings for more of a social visit. Graeme had become used to seeing Jonathan in the incubator and started his waving and cooing tactics again while he stood at the window.

A week went by and the doctors seemed pleased with the fact that Jonathan had been keeping food down without any trouble. They were starting to look more relaxed and Jonathan was definitely looking stronger. It wasn't a sudden change from one day to the next, but slowly Jonathan started to move differently. He wasn't exactly kicking his legs, but he was moving them. His eyes were more open, but he couldn't have been described as alert. Another week went by in much the same way, with me there for all the feeds and all of us there for the evening visits. The family had been visiting regularly, particularly over weekends and the hospital had become a gathering place for both our families. They all watched while Jonathan made a slow but steady recovery. My friends often met me in the hospital cafeteria for a cup of coffee before or after feeding time, because I was never home long enough to see anyone.

Day by day Jonathan grew stronger. One morning when I arrived at the ward I found that he had had his pipes and tubes removed and was awake and looking around. He was waving his arms with the jerky movements of a newborn, and kicking his legs. I knew that morning that we'd turned the corner – he had been moving around quite a lot during the week and making quite a din from time to time, but seeing him without all the attachments made me realise that the worst was over.

Chapter 9

Jonathan was a month old and he'd been in the neonatal unit for most of that time. I sometimes wonder whether, if he'd been born at full term, we would all have been spared the pain of that month.

He was still being tube fed, but I was doing a lot more for him in the way of changing and dressing. Dr Judd arrived to do his rounds one Monday morning and I was thrilled to hear him say to the sister in charge, 'I don't think Jonathan needs the incubator and we'll try bottle feeds from today and see how it goes.' He then came over and shared the wonderful news with me and I registered that he was calling the baby 'Jonathan'. He had a name; he was now a person with an identity!

After I had finished dressing Jonathan, I sat and held him as I always did after feeds and was delighted to see the incubator being wheeled away and a portable crib pushed into its place. His name card was removed from the incubator and placed at the head of his crib. A while later I wrapped him up in the blue blanket I was given and put him down to sleep. I literally skipped out of the unit and went directly to the hospital payphone to call Barry and tell him the good news. I couldn't wait for visiting time that evening when Barry and Graeme could see Jonathan in his new bed, which I could now push closer to the window so that they had an even better view.

I wanted to be back at the hospital well before the lunchtime feed, so that I could change Jonathan and talk him through what I sensed was not going to be his favourite activity – feeding from a bottle. When I got there he was crying which was hopefully an indication that he was hungry. I picked him up and rocked him until he stopped crying, and then put him on the changing table to change his nappy. He was kicking his legs madly and waving his arms and I was sure he was hungry. A challenge I had not yet considered was the changing of nappies with only one hand, but, as with so many other things I had mastered in the last twenty months, it soon came naturally to me. However, this soon paled into insignificance alongside the other difficulties I was experiencing. In fact, there was a time a few years later when I even started using cloth nappies and a nappy pin. Neither of us ever got pricked and I never stopped to try to work out how to do it; I just did it.

His nappy was changed and I was able to stand up and hold Jonathan, something I had previously not been able to do due either to my surgical wound or his tubes and paraphernalia. The bottle of formula was brought to me and I sat down on a chair near his crib, and with him in a feeding position, tried to feed him. It soon became clear that he did not know what to do and had no idea that he was supposed to suck and swallow. He pulled away every time the bottle came anywhere near his mouth. The sister was standing behind me, looking over my shoulder. She suggested I

70

squeeze the bottle slightly and squirt some formula into his mouth. With that, he choked and spluttered, spraying baby formula all over himself and me. I tried again more gently but the same thing happened. I held the teat in his mouth, hoping that he would realise it was food, but he wasn't interested and clearly did not know how to drink. Why would he want to at that stage? He had had his food delivered straight to his stomach for some time. I wondered whether instinct would take over if starvation was imminent.

Mothers always think their babies are going to starve to death and feel distressed when they won't feed. They take it as a sign of incompetence on their part and I left the ward that day in tears after having to hand over Jonathan's feeding to the sister. I felt I had failed and because I was attaching so much importance to the task of feeding him, I decided that I would watch while Jonathan was being fed at lunchtime. I got there early, feeling a little upset about what had happened earlier, and held Jonathan before his next ordeal. He smelt of baby powder and had obviously been bathed since I saw him last, I suppose as a result of the milk shower he had given us both.

I felt vindicated when the sister trying to feed him had the same problem I had experienced, but felt quite desperate that he did not have that basic human instinct to suck. The same battle ensued, with Jonathan showing absolutely no interest in taking in food. If he had been a robust-looking child perhaps it would not have seemed so crucial, but he was scrawny and wan, and looked in desperate need of a good meal. The attempt to feed him resulted in milk formula ending up everywhere, except down Jonathan's throat. There was no alternative but to tube feed him again. I must admit

71

I felt frustrated at that point, and irritated that he was being given an opportunity that he wasn't taking. It was an irrational thought, since the definition of opportunity is 'a favourable combination of circumstances' and Jonathan was not aware of his. It first occurred to me, as I lay awake that night, that parenting Jonathan was going to be very different from the first time round and in addition it would be in slow motion. Everything was going to take just a little longer. I think God looked down on me when planning my destiny and said, 'For Liz Wickins! – A boy, Jonathan – because she's in need of patience.' Something I did not have and am still trying to gather. They say that 'to know how to wait is the secret of success'. In that case, I expect to be hugely success-ful before long.

The days went by without much change. Jonathan was almost five weeks old and there had been no progress in getting him to eat on his own. We had resorted to squirting milk formula from a syringe to the back of his throat, in the hope that the swallow reflex would kick in. It worked occasionally but often resulted in panicked choking. That led to the idea of feeding Jonathan his milk with a spoon, a tactic often used for babies with a cleft palate. Using a tea-spoon seemed to keep his tongue down and acted as an irritant to the back of the mouth, resulting in a swallowing reflex. That was how Jonathan first started eating.

He became used to having his milk from a spoon and it was a good day if he took twenty-five millilitres that way. He was tube fed between spoon-feeds because he was not taking in enough, but we were teaching him day by day how to swallow and cope with food. I began to understand that nothing should be taken for granted – hence the excited phone calls, 'He's eating, he took five millilitres from a spoon today!' Every little step was a miracle, every bit of progress remarkable. The most basic human instinct, which very few parents would ever have to think about, became an achievement for Jonathan. He could swallow.

Each day Jonathan looked stronger and feeding became less and less of an ordeal. The most successful way of feeding him was via a tube to the stomach, but that was not teaching him anything. He choked and coughed his way through spoon-feeds, fighting less and accepting more readily that we were not giving up on the idea. The doctor had said that if Jonathan was able to survive without tube feeding there was no reason why he couldn't go home. That motivated me to try harder and harder, persevering through milk showers and screaming sessions, to encourage him to eat. Because feeding him by spoon wasn't enough to sustain him, we needed to get him drinking from a bottle before taking him home could even be considered. The moment had come to try again with bottle-feeding, and I was given a prepared bottle of twenty-five millilitres of a special milk formula to feed to him.

I braced myself as I approached the challenge, silently imploring him to cooperate. I put the bottle in his mouth and he merely gagged. I squeezed the bottle gently – I had learnt the consequences of being too heavy-handed – and enough milk was released for him to gurgle and splutter on before he swallowed it. The fact that he was swallowing meant that this was the route to take and the twenty-five millilitres all went down during that feed. Lessons were learnt by both Jonathan and me during the hour it took to feed him, the most important one for Jonathan being that if there was just the right amount of milk formula in his mouth at a time, he could swallow it. That lesson was an important one for his immediate progress, but the lesson for me was far more lasting, it was another exercise in patience. It is not something you are born with, it is a learnt response to life's lessons. Under the circumstances, I was getting extra lessons in patience, what with handling Jonathan and coping with the recent loss of my arm. The loss of a limb is often equated to the loss of a loved one in terms of the mourning process that must take place. Even the least vain person would feel mutilated and highly sensitive to their altered appearance. Added to this is the embarrassment and humiliation that goes with the loss of dexterity.

Jonathan would never need to be tube fed again. His feeds progressed from squeezing milk into his mouth, to making a large hole in the teat of the bottle to allow the milk to flow. He constantly choked and coughed through feeds, but slowly learnt that this was his lifeline. Occasionally he tried, unsuccessfully, to latch onto the teat, making a sucking sound, which was always followed by a spray of the formula that had rushed out of the large hole in the teat too quickly.

The doctors had set a prerequisite – when Jonathan no longer needed to be tube fed, he could go home. At long last, out came the special little white outfit that had been laundered since the last time he had almost worn it. It was time for Jonathan to learn about 'home' and 'family'.

Chapter 10

We took Jonathan home on a Saturday. New parents will know how it feels to carry your new baby into its new home. You can multiply that feeling tenfold when your child has nearly died. I remember holding Jonathan and walking with him from room to room, while Graeme gave a running commentary on what each room was used for. 'This is my room, Jonathan.' Graeme's tone towards Jonathan has never changed. The content of what he talks about now is different, but his manner and tone have always remained that of an interested, caring and totally committed brother. I knew what Graeme's next question that day was going to be. 'If I sit down, can I hold Jonny, Mom?' I was delighted to put Jonathan in Graeme's arms, his little three-year-old arms were safe and loving and so touchingly grown-up. Graeme was ecstatic, and made a big point of keeping his elbows together, remembering my joke in the hospital.

Barry kept a low profile during Jonathan's homecoming. When children are born, mothers and fathers view their birth as a joy for different reasons. As I see it, mothers generally view their children as a gift that will thrive on love and nurturing and will ultimately make them proud when they grow up to be well-adjusted adults. Fathers, on the other hand, fast-forward through the nurturing stage and picture their children, particularly their sons, as a projection of themselves. Either as they are or as they would like to be; strong and successful people who will bring pride and honour to the family. When a child with a disability is born, a father's aspirations can be shattered. I think this shattering can often be misconstrued as being connected to a damaged ego. What a shame it would be to summarily dismiss it as a pride issue, when there are so many deep-seated concerns that bear thinking about. It is at that point that reality is so painful, because he has not yet formed a relationship with the child to draw upon. It must have been incredibly painful for Barry to come to terms with the fact that Jonathan would never drive a car or play rugby, the things that most sons do. Only later would that be offset against the things that Barry came to love about Jonathan, such as his incorruptible innocence, his ability to love without question and the fact that a malicious thought would never cross his mind.

We took photographs of all of us holding Jonathan in turn and he then started to remind us that it was time for his feed. I needed to sterilise the bottles and get the formula made, so by the time his bottle was ready, he was making loud noises about the delay. Barry had gone to the pharmacy the previous day and had bought the bottles and teats that I needed. I hoped that by some miracle Jonathan would start drinking from the new bottle without any complications, but I was reminded of his frustration at not being able to suck and had to leave him screaming several times while I adjusted the size of the hole in the teat. It took days to get the feeding conditions just right for him; the chair in his room was a favourite and a particular teat worked best. His love for music was born in those very early days and he became noticeably more relaxed when music was played during his feeds. Although Jonathan was taking food more willingly and more effectively, he was not eating enough to last him several hours, so nights were a problem. I was getting up to feed him every two to three hours. Both Graeme and Jonathan were born during the winter months and getting out of a warm bed at night to feed Jonathan was something I could have done without. Perhaps it was because Graeme was our first child that Barry was so involved in his night-time feeds, or maybe this was how Barry showed his subconscious indifference to Jonathan being at home. It makes me smile when I think about using the word 'indifferent' to describe Barry's attitude towards Jonathan today. If I could think of a word that aptly describes the opposite of 'indifferent', it would perfectly define his attitude towards Jonathan today.

It always amazes me how households adjust to major changes and more responsibilities and tasks are crammed into already busy lives. I think this is why it is true that there is no ideal time to start a family. You work around the birth of your children; your life does not stop as a result, it changes. The change is not only connected to your lifestyle, but also to the way you view the world; there is now an extension of yourself to consider and to fit into the world you had previously shaped to suit yourself.

Jonathan continued to feed well and had even started to suck when he was very hungry. He was feeding every two hours, both night and day, which was tiring and the lack of sleep was wearing me down. He often didn't settle after feeds and because I was so protective of him when he was first at home, I couldn't walk away from him unless he was sound asleep. My sister-in-law visited us one afternoon and promised to talk to her sister about giving me a wind-up swaying crib that her child had outgrown. It was soon delivered and should have arrived with bows and ribbons and bottles of champagne attached to it, because it turned out to be the best gift I have ever received. I don't know how I would have coped without it.

Jonathan has always found comfort in routine and he soon fell into a pattern of being fed, changed and winded, and he then settled down to be rocked to sleep in his swinging cradle. While the cradle clicked to and fro, I was temporarily given my life back to do the basic things which are often taken for granted, such as having a bath or washing and drying my hair. Despite the fact that I was tired and rushed, I often stood watching Jonathan sleep as he swung backwards and forwards, his face pushed up towards the side of the cradle. The sides were made of a type of net fabric so watching him was easy. Watching him had become easy anyway, because I just loved him more and more each day.

The local provincial hospital ran a clinic for babies with intellectual disabilities. Mothers could take their babies there once a month for expert advice from a physiotherapist, an occupational therapist and a speech therapist. I walked into the hospital building holding Jonathan, not knowing where to go or what to expect. I was directed to a therapy hall which had a large padded mat in the centre. By the time I had filled in the forms and given Jonathan's birth history, many mothers had gathered and were seated on the mat with their babies. Once I'd settled down and began to look around, the shock of seeing so many children with obvious physical abnormalities flung me headlong into a world that

I didn't feel I belonged to and didn't want to be a part of. I was suddenly overcome by one of the most powerful emotions I had ever experienced. My eyes darted frantically around the mat and if I'd had the strength I would have picked Jonathan up and run. The reality of the sadness of mental disability was only apparent to me through someone else's child, not my own. Surely that supports the theory that love is blind?

I battled my way through that first session, concentrating more on maintaining my composure than administering therapy to Jonathan. At those sessions I made good friends and was taught many valuable things about handling a disabled child, but it took several months for me to feel comfortable about being there. It was on that very mat that Jonathan's uncooperative and stubborn tendencies first started peeping through the cracks. If I wanted his head one way, he wanted it the other way. When we got home and the pressure was off, Jonathan turned himself inside out to impress me. I was actually always impressed, but I was starting to think that the therapists at the clinic thought I was going through a process of denial, constantly claiming that Jonathan could do certain things that they had never seen him do. That is a lesson that the years with Jonathan have taught me: it really isn't important what other people think.

The months flew by, bringing better success with feeding. Jonathan slowly started eating mashed food, choking and spitting as he had first done with milk formula but I knew he would get the hang of it in due course. I marvelled every day at how he'd learnt to suck his bottle. Sucking the bottle was never a quiet process because Jonathan's mouth was not a normal shape, and in the still of the night it sounded like the noise our swimming pool pump made when the water level got too low. I remember Graeme sometimes being awake as a result of the noise, when I was feeding Jonathan at night.

Barry is now able to admit freely that he felt enormous sub-conscious anger, confusion and resentment at having been given a disabled child. He had no interest in holding Jonathan or helping me with him, and focused all his love and attention on Graeme. His hugely demonstrative love for Graeme created a very painful contrast that alienated me – I felt tossed aside and cordoned off into a corner with Jonathan that was a no-go area. Our marriage was placed under tremendous strain and required a great deal of work over time to mend. A lot had happened in my life during those years and I was not as understanding to Barry's needs as I should have been, perhaps because I selfishly presumed mine were more pressing. I wish it were possible to go back and make it all better and do things with the twenty-twenty vision of hindsight, not that the end result would have been any different. Barry grew to love Jonathan with the deepest love, the strongest loyalty and the fiercest protection.

Chapter 11

Jonathan reached milestones in his own time and at his own pace. No two people are alike, and the same applies to people with Down syndrome. Jonathan smiled when he was four months old, held his head up on his own at nine months, sat up at fifteen months, and walked when he was four years old. One should bear in mind that this is a story about Jonathan and not about people with Down syndrome in general. I can imagine the buzz from protesting parents of children with Down syndrome shouting, 'Rubbish, my child sat at six months and walked at fourteen months.' As I have already said, there are no textbook cases, and Jonathan, like all children, proceeded at his own pace. What possible difference would it have made if he had walked at two years instead of four, other than the inconvenience of carrying him? We would still be where we are today and it made no difference, but at the time every improvement was a great incentive to remain focused on his ability to reach full potential.

The word potential means 'latent but unrealised ability', so in this context it relates to the highest level of ability that a child could possibly and ultimately reach. If you wanted to measure potential according to mental age, which is never a good measure, but makes the concept easier to understand, you could say that Jonathan has the potential of a mental age of a twelve-year-old. That would mean that I, or anyone else making these very subjective predictions, would expect Jonathan at his peak to be functioning at the level of a twelve-year-old genetically normal child. I have never liked predicting potential and view it with scepticism. It is a form of labelling and I could write another book on how damaging labelling can be. It is more productive not to worry about the long-term potential of the child, but rather to concentrate on making sure that the opportunity to learn each step is taken so it can be mastered and achieved. That is the principle of the early intervention system, used by most developed countries to get the greatest possible developmental outcomes from mentally challenged children in their early years. There are programmes available in this country based on the early intervention principles and most pre-school facilities follow its guidelines.

When Jonathan first smiled at four months it was confirmation that he was going to reach all the milestones he was supposed to, but was going to do so later than most children. When you have to wait for something, it is less likely to be taken for granted. I think a baby's first smile is the reward for the sacrifices that have been made since its birth. The waking up at night, the constant feeding and changing is now rewarded. That smile also makes everything you do thereafter even more of a pleasure. Unfortunately during this time it was a pleasure I enjoyed alone. Jonathan started smiling and hasn't really stopped and his smiles seem to light up his face. He doesn't walk or run well and his speech is not very clear to others, but his smiles brighten up a whole room.

We all know, approximately, when genetically normal children are expected to smile, sit, crawl, walk and talk for the first time. For children with Down syndrome this can vary from child to child and because their milestones cannot be predicted, when they do actually occur, all the bells ring.

It was a long time before Jonathan could sit. He spent most of his waking hours during the day on a rug on the floor. The therapy sessions had shown me how to encourage him to pull himself up. I had covered a foam roll, similar to the one we used at the hospital, and I put him over it, facedown, a few times a day, with his legs on the floor at the back and his chest and arms over the roll. The idea was that he would develop the strength in his neck to hold his head up unaided. He spent many months examining, at very close range, the design of the fabric I had used to cover the roll. Graeme and I would lie down on the floor in front of him and get up to all sorts of antics in the hope that he would lift his head to see what we were up to. Eventually he did, at nine months. We had been doing exercises every day to strengthen his poor muscle tone, a problem most people with Down syndrome have. It was a game for Graeme and one that Jonathan didn't seem to mind playing. Graeme's favourite was when we crossed Jonathan's legs over each other when he was lying on his back and turned him on his side hoping he would push himself onto his front and learn to roll over. Before he mastered it he often got into knots with his legs and arms in the wrong place, which resulted in shrieks of mirth from Graeme.

The most vivid memory I have of Jonathan at that age is of him lying on his back on a rug looking at his fingers. He had discovered he had five of them on each hand and was fascinated that they could move. He literally spent hours looking at the back of one of his hands. Occasionally he would fall asleep, probably mesmerised by the moving fingers, and his hand would drop and hit him in the face. The fright always upset him and he would cry and need consoling, heartbroken that his fingers could do that to him. Once he had mastered rolling over and holding his head up, he found a new position to view the world and his fingers. He was now able to lie on his stomach, pull himself up onto his elbows and assess his surroundings. He often lay in that position examining his fingers, but had also grown to love a toy my sister Margaret had given him. It was a toy television set that, when wound up, played a tune and rolled a picture across the screen. He adored it and spent hours lying on his stomach watching the picture and listening to the music. It required constant winding with some gentle and some not so gentle reminders from Jonathan if he thought it was taking too long. His grasp improved over time and soon he was able to lie on his back and hold the toy at arm's length in order to see the picture. That had even more disastrous consequences when he nodded off to sleep.

Jonathan experienced bouts of pneumonia in the first year of his life. I remember racing to the hospital with a blue baby in the middle of the night, terrified that he would stop breathing. This was not restricted to the first year, however, but continued throughout Jonathan's life, being at its worst when he was about three years old.

My sister Pat regularly regaled the family with a satirical 'newsletter' concerning the activities of family members. No one escaped her acid comments, and Jonathan was no exception. We had scheduled his official baptism on four separate occasions which all had to be cancelled because of his hospitalisation at the last minute. Pat reported that Jonathan was guilty of insubordination and contempt for not attending important family functions, namely his own baptism, which raised a good laugh during difficult times. It had been much easier to arrange his first baptism in hospital than the official gathering he kept avoiding, but we eventually pulled it off when he was six months old.

Jonathan still occasionally gets pneumonia, like last winter when he played 'call back the past' and scared us all half to death. Jonathan is unique in so many ways, but the way he gets sick so quickly is very 'him'. He gets desperately ill within hours and does the same when he turns the corner to recovery. He just snaps back to being his old self, while we walk around with knees like jelly, still reeling from the shock.

Jonathan had a bigger tongue than most other babies with Down syndrome and I had been advised to consider a tongue reduction operation for him because he seemed to be choking at night. A doctor suggested that his feeding problem might be a result of the size of his tongue. I did as much research as I possibly could, and after much soul-searching, decided to proceed with the surgery. While the surgeon was discussing the operation with me, he asked me if I wanted to have any cosmetic surgery done to Jonathan at the same time. This can entail building up the bridge of the nose, straightening the eyes, and generally giving the child a more 'normal' appearance. I feel this puts the child at a severe disadvantage, as societal expectations would be for him then to behave 'normally'. Apart from this, I would never consider putting a child, especially a sickly one, through the trauma of unnecessary surgery. I really like the way people with

Down syndrome look; from the first glimpse of their faces, no presumptions or unrealistic expectations are made.

Our marriage had hit its lowest point by the time of Jonathan's operation. When the difficult decision, with incalculable results, had to be made, I was left feeling lonely, frightened, resentful and terribly uncertain about whether I had made the right choice or not. The procedure entailed cutting a triangular wedge from the tip of the tongue and then rejoining the tongue. I was warned that it could be a painful procedure, so I was delighted to find that, after a day's initial discomfort, Jonathan's tongue healed remarkably quickly.

There were four months between my decision to go ahead with the operation, and the operation actually taking place. During this time, Jonathan was propped up into a sitting position, and while in this position, his tongue lolled forward and appeared to be even larger than I had first thought. Whether it had actually grown, or was just more visible in this position was impossible to tell, but it strengthened my resolve to go ahead with the operation.

The operation was done when Jonathan was fourteen months old, with all the usual trauma and anxiety associated with hospital stays. People have since asked my advice about tongue reduction, but I am unable to offer a firm opinion. It is impossible to measure what benefit, if any, Jonathan gained. However, I am pleased that I found the courage to do it, particularly when I occasionally see a person with Down syndrome with an overly big tongue, with sores around their mouth and a wet chest from dribbling.

Jonathan was a delightful child when he was about sixteen

months old and had a permanent smile on his face and a constant chuckle. This was when Barry started to notice him. It was very hard not to, as he laughed incessantly, lighting up the space around him. We had started propping him up with large cushions to encourage him to sit. Just when we thought he was getting the hang of it, he would adopt what we called the 'leaning tower' position which normally led to the 'drop down', onto the shoulder with his arm trapped underneath him. He was so good-natured at that age and would simply lie there until he was propped up again. If the cushions were too high behind him, he would occasionally drop face down on the floor, his head between his legs – a move a gymnast would be proud of but one Jonathan did not enjoy.

Barry's succumbing to Jonathan's charms was not an overnight event, but a slow process. It was during this time that our marriage was in serious trouble and I had started taking some painful steps to deal with the problems we were experiencing. Rightly or wrongly, I started leaving both children with Barry for periods of time over the weekends, in the hope that he would start becoming more involved with Jonathan. Luckily, this was exactly what happened. Without Barry even being aware of it, Jonathan was working his magic and I found Barry voluntarily becoming more and more involved with both of the children. He would put Jonathan in his bouncy chair to feed him and from then on Jonathan spent a lot of time in his chair around Barry, being moved from place to place to be near him. It was at this time that a transformation seemed to be taking place – it was no longer childminding; he was being moved around because Barry wanted to be with him and talk to him. Barry had started taking over Jonathan's feeding, which was always easier on the kitchen counter because of his height and because Jonathan liked the face to face contact. There was no mistaking when it was Jonathan's lunchtime over the weekends because of the nursery rhymes and songs that came from the kitchen, with Graeme joining in the chorus. I find it difficult to describe the overwhelming relief and gladness I felt, listening to the three of them, after all we had been through. Barry became more and more involved with Jonathan and his relationship was beginning to resemble the one he had with Graeme when he was a tiny baby.

The months went by and Barry's and my relationship began to strengthen. We were beginning to share the responsibility of Jonathan. Marriage problems often take as long to put right as they do to deteriorate, but we were heading in the right direction. I have photographs of a family holiday around that time and they are happy pictures of us all. Some of those pictures represent the turning point in Barry's relationship with Jonathan. The picture of Jonathan sitting on Barry's chest was taken on that holiday and the look on Barry's face could not be mistaken for anything but paternal love.

I had been going to the hospital therapy sessions every month and when Jonathan was about a year old, we were chosen to participate in a programme that was being offered to a few families in the group. I think our family was chosen because of my physical disability and they probably also realised that I had not been getting sufficient support or physical help at home, as many of the exercises required another pair of hands. It may also have been because Jonathan was lagging behind the other children with Down syndrome of the same age. It is human nature to compare children's abilities, but under the circumstances, it is unkind and unwise. Some of the children his age were already crawling and Jonathan was not even sitting yet, which made me terribly despondent. I'm sure that by the time they were all five years old, they were doing exactly the same things and I wish I had realised that at the time.

I made the big mistake of thinking that the ability of a child with Down syndrome was linked to the effort put into their training and care. I had never been told that they were not all born the same. I had no concept of a mild, severe or profound disability when it came to categorising them. I think that is why it was so hard for me to see other children with Down syndrome doing so much better than Jonathan – I thought I was not trying hard enough.

My feelings of inadequacy also stemmed from the fact that there had been several television programmes about the lives of people with Down syndrome. I had not been aware in the early years of Jonathan's life that there was a condition called Mosaic Down syndrome, which is different from the typical condition. In this instance, nature's error occurs slightly later and only after some cells have replicated normally. Therefore, only some of the child's cells have the extra chromosome, while the rest do not. These children often have the same physical characteristics as children with the typical condition, but function at a much higher level and quite often can be close to within the normal range. It is a rare form of Down syndrome and only represents approximately one per cent of all people with the syndrome. Obviously when looking for people with Down syndrome to act in films, or represent the condition, Mosaics are used because they have the typical appearance, but can talk intelligibly and remember their lines. Although any form of contact between society and Down syndrome is desirable and opens the doors to understanding, it can create major disappointment for the other ninety-nine per cent of parents. No matter how hard they have worked with their full-blown Down syndrome child, they will never attain the same level of proficiency. It is not the actual differences between the children that hurts the parents, as most of them become aware of Mosaic Down syndrome at some stage, but the comparison made by the public, who are led to believe that all people with Down syndrome operate at this higher level. It creates an impression that with the correct care and training, the same could be achieved with all Down syndrome people, the inference being that the parents of a non-Mosaic hadn't put in as much effort.

The person appointed by the hospital to counsel our family was a pleasant and well-qualified nursing sister called Estelle. She spent a couple of hours in the afternoon once a week in our home. Jonathan had become uncooperative and disruptive at the hospital therapy sessions, and that could probably also be added to the list of possible reasons that our family was chosen for home therapy. Estelle's weekly visits helped me in so many more ways than just administering therapy and showing me the exercises appropriate to Jonathan's development. She seemed to understand how all our family members were involved with Jonathan and cared about us all. Because of her medical background, I was able to phone her for advice when Jonathan was sick. She was a counsellor and a good friend, providing the necessary support where support was lacking during the year she was assigned to our case.

Chapter 12

Once Jonathan was able to sit up, life changed so much for him. He could be in a sit-up pushchair and see where he was going but I don't think he really grasped that as the adventure, he just wanted to be on the move. If I dared stop the pushchair to talk to someone, he objected loudly. I took him with me to most places and the tinkle of the car keys was the cue that we were going out. If I was leaving him with Barry, I made sure I didn't rattle my keys.

Now that he was sitting, it was time for Jonathan to interact with children of his own age. I went to the Sunshine Centre, which is a pre-school facility offering an early intervention programme for mentally challenged children. They were able to take him after the July school holidays, as he was almost eighteen months old by then.

The Sunshine Centre's school building was at the top of a long and very steep path. Like many parents in the school, I had to carry Jonathan up that hill every morning before he started walking at the age of four. The first morning I carried him up the path to the flat playground area in front of the building, it was before official school hours and many of the children were on the playground. When I had previously visited the school the children were in their classrooms, so I had not seen any of them. I had not expected to feel the way I did as I stood there clinging onto Jonathan, rather than him clinging onto me. The same feeling of emotional turmoil came over me as I had felt when I saw the children at our first therapy session and it surprised me that I felt so traumatised.

Children generally stayed at the Sunshine Centre until they were six or seven years old, when it was then time for them to move on to formal education. I think seeing the older children upset me and reminded me of the reality of our future. Perhaps I had not allowed myself to think that this was a long-term arrangement that lasted beyond babyhood. Or perhaps disabilities become more evident as children get older and I was seeing severely disabled children for the first time. It became clear to me then how unfair it is that physical disabilities quite often accompany a mental disability. You'd think one was enough, but I suppose in some cases one could be the result of the other. Looking at it from a different perspective, perhaps it is kinder for a profoundly physically disabled child not to be able to comprehend his other tragic circumstances. Whatever it was that shocked me on Jonathan's first day of school never affected me again, but I drove home after spending the day with him in the classroom, with tears streaming down my face. It is frightening and disconcerting to see severely disabled children and to come to the realisation that your child belongs with them. This is a very normal reaction, and now that I know these children so well, I can honestly say that I no longer see their disabilities.

I left Jonathan at school the next day and every school day

after that for close on six years, apart from the year he spent at home. Being with other children created the problem of his contracting infections and he was plagued by chest problems for the first year he was there. Jonathan had been in hospital with pneumonia so regularly that the paediatrician had strongly recommended that we keep him on a maintenance dose of an antibiotic for a year. He was better on the antibiotic, but we had to reassess the situation when he developed a collapsed lung and septicaemia and did not respond so readily to increased antibiotic treatment.

Lunchtime was always a problem for Jonathan and the staff at school. He wasn't feeding himself yet and was still on quite a sloppy diet at home, where we had calm times between sickly spells and were not allowing them to be spoilt by constant fighting about food. As soon as we tried to introduce anything with a different texture, he would choke and so we would stick with the food that worked for him. There was a young speech therapist, David*, at the school who attended to the children with eating difficulties, and he believed that most of Jonathan's problems were behavioural. Jonathan had become very wilful by the time he was eighteen months old, so I suppose the possibility existed that he was being bloody-minded about eating as well. In hindsight, all the pointers were there that he had a severe swallowing disorder, but I saw it as an expected difficulty due to his feeding problems from the outset.

David believed that Jonathan should be firmly handled and suggested that the feeding difficulties we were having at home were probably due to incorrect handling. He said he

*Name has been changed.

could get Jonathan's feeding problem under control, and because I was feeling so exasperated, I welcomed the help. I wasn't sure how he was going to do it, but I trusted his judgement and training, as he held a doctorate in his field. What I didn't realise was that his training method entailed holding Jonathan's head in a tight grip under his arm, while food was shovelled into Jonathan's mouth and he screamed blue murder.

For a long time I picked up a distressed Jonathan after school, not realising the extent of the trauma he was being subjected to, but believing his misery stemmed from the same battle of wills being waged at home over food.

Jonathan started developing pneumonia regularly, and an X-ray revealed that he was inhaling food, probably while crying during feeding. His maintenance dose of antibiotics could not help when he aspirated some of his lunch. I arrived at the school early one day and followed the sound of screams. I was horrified at the manhandling Jonathan was being subjected to and put an immediate stop to it. There is no word for the sound a child makes when he has been crying and makes involuntary hiccup sounds. He often used to 'hic' all the way home in the car because of the trauma he was going through. On the day I found out why he was crying, I hated myself for letting him down as his mother and guardian. Each sob and 'hic' was like a knife of guilt stabbing me. I didn't know that he had a medical condition that made swallowing very hard for him.

We experienced easier times by taking the pressure off Jonathan, both at home and at school, and fed him what he could cope with. David probably saw it as yet more parental weakness that fitted in with his initial judgement of the family's overprotectiveness.

The physiotherapist at the school was working with Jonathan regularly and Estelle was still making home calls. We were all encouraging Jonathan to master the next stage in his development – crawling. The word 'encouraging' sounds as if we were giving him passive inspiration but nothing was passive with Jonathan. He had always been uncooperative with therapy and whined through all the sessions. We had become a bit immune to his complaints and carried on doing what we thought would be good for him, even if he didn't agree. Despite the fact that Jonathan has always had extremely low muscle tone, he has incredible physical strength and he could put up a world-class fight. Some of his most famous struggles at that age were during haircuts. The barber I had been taking him to suggested that in future I make the last appointment of the day for Jonathan, so that he could close the shop while he cut his hair. I think the message was clear: Jonathan was scaring the customers! That didn't surprise me; I was pretty scared too.

This must have been the point where I stood back and took a long, hard look at myself. I was thirty-five years old and this can often be an age of assessment of how 'on track' you think your life is, compared to where you thought you'd be at that stage. I don't fully understand the reasons I decided to take up studying psychology at that time. It could have been that I needed to do something for me, or in order to break out of the mould I'd cast myself in, or it may have been because I really wanted to know more about human behaviour.

Barry supported and encouraged me wholeheartedly, looking after Jonathan and making it possible for me to study. Attaining a degree in psychology required five years of dedication and sacrifice, while simultaneously coping with a very active Jonathan. On many levels, obtaining the degree allowed me to view the future more positively and served to bolster my self-esteem.

Another major motivating factor was the opportunity to learn more about Down syndrome, and I used the university library to read up on everything I could on the subject. My course also covered elementary genetics and the terms 'genes', 'chromosomes' and 'DNA' started to have more meaning for me.

Barry's relationships with Graeme and Jonathan were now on a par. He looked at Jonathan in the same adoring way he looked at Graeme. He often got up at night to attend to Jonathan and I could see his love for him grew daily. It must have been true love, because Jonathan was not always easy to handle. Barry has always known his own mind and is often intolerant of people who don't. An incident involving him and Jonathan shows the battle of wills that sometimes developed between them. Jonathan had become fascinated with the children's rides sometimes found outside super-markets. He had noticed a rocking horse and almost fell out of Barry's arms trying to get to it every time we were in the centre. As Barry took him towards it, he would cower and change his mind. This went on for months until Barry had had enough. The next time we were in the centre and Jonathan showed an interest, Barry placed him in the saddle, put the coin in the slot and the horse started moving. Jonathan started grizzling loudly, but Barry ignored him. The grizzling continued until the ride was over and Barry lifted Jonathan off. I was about to give Barry a blast when Jonathan yelled, 'More! More! More!'

At this time, Graeme was experiencing bouts of vomiting and stomach trouble that continued for some time, and resulted in him being admitted to hospital for further investigation. It transpired that he had problems with both his kidneys and would require surgery. In the first operation, the ureter was transplanted to a different place in one of his kidneys and the same operation was done three months later on the other kidney. The timing of the diagnosis of Graeme's medical problem was good, as he was due to start school the following year. He was a model five-year-old patient who would make any mother proud. Although there was some damage to one of his kidneys, he has never looked back and has been extremely healthy ever since.

The next big milestone was when Jonathan started to crawl. This turned him into a small human tornado, and our lives were never the same again. Havoc followed him closely wherever he went, either creeping along the ground or climbing out of places that no longer contained him. He crawled for about two years before he walked and was very hard to keep up with towards the end of his crawling days. One would literally have to run alongside him to keep up. Jonathan had always had a reflux problem and usually brought up a bit of his milk after feeds. It became very easy to keep track of where he was in the house because you could follow the trail of regurgitated milk puddles that stained our carpets.

The feeding problems had taken on new proportions. Jonathan became very excited at the sight of food and flapped his arms in anticipation but as the spoon approached his mouth, he would either bang his head against the wall behind him or crash his head into the bowl of food in front of him. Crying and wriggling out of the bottom of his high chair accompanied these traumatic mealtimes. The school was having the same difficulties and at the annual assessment meeting the issue of his general behaviour, and more particularly his feeding, came under discussion. David, the speech therapist, was at the meeting and seized the opportunity to once again suggest that this was a case of parental mismanagement. The professional staff at the meeting decided that the only course open to them was to send Jonathan to Tara, a provincial psychiatric hospital, for assessment.

In general, constructive criticism is not only welcome, but necessary. However one will always come across people who have strong opinions that they will voice loudly, based on what they know about 'normal' children. But even well-meant criticism can be difficult to accept.

Chapter 13

Taking Jonathan to Tara for an assessment made me feel that I had failed as a mother. The social worker at the Sunshine Centre who referred us had mentioned that parents might be observed interacting with their children through a one-way mirror. I had great difficulty with this and despite the fact that there was no such facility there, the idea made me think that my behaviour was under scrutiny, not Jonathan's. It is very difficult to have to put your feelings and emotions 'on show', particularly when you have in your mind, albeit wrongly, that it is you they are trying to pinpoint as the cause of the problem. When I use the term 'they', I think I had visions of doctors in white coats carrying large bunches of keys, waiting for me to make a slip that would reveal I was the guilty party.

Barry, Jonathan and I were taken to a small consultation room with chairs arranged in a circle. We arrived first and people then started to wander in. They were not wearing white coats and they did not look threatening in any way. Once everyone had arrived, the psychiatrist in charge opened Jonathan's file and read the referral letter from the school. She looked up over her glasses and said to Barry, 'Why do you think you are here?' This was a clever approach because she wanted to know from him whether we were there because we felt we needed help or because the school had sent us. He glanced at me uncertainly and replied, 'The school says Jonathan won't eat.' I would have given the same answer. Was it denial or loyalty to Jonathan that we had to be encouraged to admit that we were having major difficulties with him?

The various professionals on the panel asked us questions about what was happening at home and we slowly opened up, answering only what we were asked and not volunteering much more. Jonathan was in his pushchair and had been whinging to get out and started to make quite a noise. I picked him up and he wriggled out of my arms onto the floor and crawled around, pulling himself up onto anything he could reach to pull down. The bottle of soap on the basin crashed to the floor and as he grabbed at the towel on the rail, he lost his balance and fell over. The psychiatrist looked at me and said, 'You understand, Mrs Wickins, that this meeting will not be productive while Jonathan is here. I would like him to be removed and cared for by the staff. Are you okay with that?' I nodded, wondering how the staff would cope and whether they would keep him safe.

The school staff believed Jonathan needed behaviour modification and had indicated the feeding problem as their main concern. The psychologist on the panel had said that the banging of his head against the wall was a major concern and could indicate psychological disturbance. Jonathan had also started hitting himself in the face when confronted with food and that added to their concerns. The social worker recommended that a programme be drawn up to address the difficulties we were having with Jonathan and the various professionals started making copious notes on how to implement it. The psychiatrist then asked about Jonathan's feeding history in more detail and wrote down our replies in the file. She closed the file and looked up at Barry and me and said, 'Okay, we would be happy to put Jonathan into a behaviour modification programme, but there are a few things I want before we proceed. Firstly, I want him to see a paediatric surgeon, and secondly, I want him to be observed here for a full day. I also want him to have an EEG. We will meet again once that has happened and take it from there.'

I didn't know what 'being put into a programme' really meant and I didn't ask for details because I wasn't sure I wanted to know. Did 'put in' mean he would have to stay there? I fretted about that, but didn't want to show resistance because I really needed help with a situation that had become completely untenable.

I made arrangements for Jonathan to spend the day at Tara that week and to have the EEG done on a different day. I also booked an appointment with a paediatric surgeon for the following week. The pleasant young girl who was given the task of observing Jonathan at Tara looked a lot more energetic in the morning than when I fetched him later that afternoon.

There's nothing more tiring and exasperating than being responsible for a hyperactive child who is taken out of his usual environment and put into a totally new one with new avenues to explore. I knew that from attempting to socialise with my friends who had genetically normal children of the same age, and feeling that if this was socialising, I'd rather be a recluse. One day while visiting a friend at her home,

Jonathan got stuck in the fireplace, while attempting to climb up the chimney. He wasn't walking yet, so he'd pull himself up on anything he came across, having little sense about what was dangerous and what wasn't. As I reached into the fireplace to pull him out I was deafened by his echoed scream of fright as he realised it was dark and unfamiliar up there. I decided it was time to go home once I'd prised him out and we were both covered in soot.

The EEG was to be done at Tara and Barry and I were both there, knowing from our trips to the hospital when Jonathan had pneumonia what we were in for. The EEG was a whole lot worse. An EEG is an electroencephalogram and it observes the characteristic pattern of recorded brainwaves. Electrodes are attached to the scalp to record the pattern and to do this Jonathan needed to be sedated. The sedative made him fight like a lion instead of calming him down. Ruffling his hair was a major intrusion on his senses, now we were attaching suction pads to his head and he wasn't having it. It was a long three hours and I've never been sure that the results of that EEG were worth having because of the test circumstances.

I took Jonathan to the paediatric surgeon the following week and he listened intently to the problems we'd been having. His immediate response, with no question in his mind, from what he had heard from me, was that Jonathan had a swallowing dysfunction. He was so certain about it so early on in our conversation that it must have been blatantly obvious. Why had so many people missed it, myself included? The only way to find out exactly what the problem was and how to treat it was for the doctor to put Jonathan under anaesthetic and have a look.

Barry and I waited outside the operating theatre, ready to pounce on the surgeon for information. He emerged nodding, 'Yes,' he said, 'he is not able to swallow easily, he has a valve problem.' He went on to tell us that Jonathan also had a severe reflux problem and because he hadn't been eating regularly, acid was forming in his stomach and being regurgitated into his oesophagus. This had caused the oesophagus to become ulcerated and raw, making the swallowing of food absolute agony. No wonder he was hitting himself in the face and banging his head on the wall. He was starving, but knew the consequences if he were to swallow. It was terribly upsetting to recall the constant fight to make him eat and I felt awful, but at the same time I was hugely relieved that the problem had been identified.

Nothing could be done about the swallowing dysfunction other than to slowly reintroduce food that Jonathan liked and which would easily slip down his throat. The doctor recommended that I thicken his milk with baby porridge before he went to bed at night, in the hope that he would sleep longer. He said quite seriously, 'You may be giving Jonathan porridge on his twenty-first birthday, so get used to it.' Like so many things in human development it was a wait-and-see situation. The valve could strengthen with normal development or it could remain the same. In fact, Jonathan started eating solid food when he was about eight years old, gagging regularly and often not keeping it down. If only we could have known at the time that one of his greatest pleasures would one day become food! Today he eats anything that is put in front of him and does so with skill and good table manners, despite the occasional choke if he's in too much of a hurry.

We had a follow-up meeting at Tara some weeks later and it was decided that the behaviour patterns responsible for the referral were related to and explained by his medical condition. The surgeon sent me a copy of the letter he had sent to the school about Jonathan and the issue was never raised again. It was accepted that he would not progress onto the next level of eating development until he was ready to do so. The EEG, for what it was worth, showed a pattern that was not normal. The reason the psychiatrist thought an EEG was necessary was because Jonathan had been having transient episodes of a trance-like state. We still call it 'the dance of joy' because he seems to go into this state during times of pleasure, like while there is music playing or when he's travelling in a car, his two favourite activities. He would sit on the ground with his feet lifted off the floor by a couple of inches. He'd then sway his head and shoulders from side to side, creating momentum that would lift a helicopter. In the car the space restriction didn't put him off, although it's a bit of a problem these days. I always marvel at how strong his stomach muscles must have been to be able to do that with his feet lifted off the ground. When he was young a bomb could have gone off next to him while he was in that state and I'm sure he wouldn't have noticed. There were suggestions that it could have been petit mal epilepsy, but I never took them seriously for two reasons. One, because I don't believe that the EEG was an accurate test or whether we would ever get one that was. And two, because to treat a person for epilepsy, one requires follow-up EEGs and I wasn't going to put him through that again.

When the psychiatrist saw us for the follow-up consultation, she asked us to come alone and she saw us independently from the rest of the team. We discussed what had happened and how we could best deal with it, and just when I thought the meeting was over she said, 'I have something else to talk about. Jonathan's case has been discussed at length and all the team members recommend, unanimously, that your family needs "time out".' The term 'time out' makes me think of a sports match and the players having a rest. I suppose that is exactly what was implied, except that this was not a game. I could see by the look on her face that she was not thinking of an afternoon's time out. She went on to say, 'We would like you to admit Jonathan to Tara for two weeks while the family has a break and we recommend that you go away on holiday with Graeme. I don't think you realise that your family is in crisis. Your lives have one purpose at the moment and that is to keep Jonathan safe, and you must have time to reflect on your own lives and spend time with each other.' I'm not sure why, but I burst into tears. Perhaps it was because she had so astutely summed up exactly what was happening in our home and it was the first time anyone had come close enough to our family to be able to make that assessment and it was a great relief. Or possibly it was the awful thought of spending time away from Jonathan, because I had previously never needed to.

Barry and I drove home in stunned silence because we knew we had to do something about the situation. The psychiatrist had mentioned Graeme and said several times that families in crisis are not functional. I think she was right in considering Graeme – he had been a little boy thrown into the adult world of responsibility. I remember the panicked look he'd get on his face if he couldn't spot his brother, even though the responsibility of keeping track of him was definitely not his. When we got home, we had tea before Barry went back to work and I went to fetch Jonathan from school. I suggested that we take a break separately. I would go away with Jonathan for a while to give Barry and Graeme a break and then Barry could take Jonathan to the coast with him, and give me a break. Barry liked that idea because he wanted this whole thing to go away – he couldn't stand the thought of Jonathan being scared in a new environment. What a wonderful and timely turnaround. We parted, promising to talk about it later that evening.

While on my way to fetch Jonathan I dwelled on what had happened that morning and it became very clear to me that we needed to take Tara's advice very seriously and have a break without Jonathan. Barry and I discussed it that night and agreed to take Graeme away. We could not face the thought of admitting Jonathan to Tara and in trying to find an alternative, Helen seemed the obvious choice.

Helen had been our housekeeper since Jonathan was very young. She knew him well and he loved her beyond question. It was not the intention, when she first started working for us, that she would be Jonathan's nanny, but she took over the role of helping me with him whenever she thought I needed help. Jonathan was not the sort of child you could have a part-relationship with. He was all encompassing – I think the term is 'in your face'. Anyone who came close to Jonathan learnt to love him and Helen was very close to him. She had been there during his illnesses and she'd seen and experienced the food wars. I trusted Helen implicitly with Jonathan. He could stay in his own surroundings, eat what he was used to eating and not have to deal with strangers. Under those conditions, we decided to take a two-week break at the coast. Helen has often talked about how all my sisters rallied around while I was away and spent time with Jonathan in the afternoons. Going out in the car with any of his aunts, and they often took him, was marked on his calendar as a very special event. He loved the car and he loved them.

The break was probably good for all of us and sleeping until one wakes was a luxury I had forgotten about. Jonathan was at home, but with us all the time. We never stopped saying 'Wouldn't Jonathan love this.' We got home refreshed and ready to face whatever lay ahead.

This time of assessment made us aware of what Jonathan meant to us. We wanted the best for him, but at the same time we were aware that in so doing, we might not be doing the best for the family. Without our family intact, we could offer him nothing. It seems strange that the more problems we had with Jonathan, the more we loved him. Perhaps that is the principle and law of unconditional love.

Jonathan continued to contract pneumonia and had a particularly bad bout of double pneumonia later that year. We knew him and the symptoms of pneumonia so well that we reacted calmly, but with great respect for the fact that Jonathan always got sick in a big hurry. Between the time we realised he was deteriorating and the time we got him to the hospital, he was often a pale shade of blue. By that time I was extremely grateful to hand him over to unflustered professionals. Those days in the hospital were exhausting. Jonathan would not stay in the oxygen tent or keep a drip in his arm without putting up a fight. When he was very ill they had to strap him down, tying his arms to the sides of the cot so that he couldn't pull the drip out. The only time he was calm under those circumstances was when he was asleep. I sometimes climbed into the oxygen tent with him in the hope that he would fall asleep in my arms, but he was always too busy trying to get out to settle for anything else.

We had trouble with pneumonia for some months after that and Jonathan spent more time either in hospital or at home than at school that year.

Chapter 14

Barry and I decided to keep Jonathan out of school for a year. I hoped to get his feeding under control in that time and also isolate him from the infections he was picking up at school. I had been reading about an early intervention programme, which I investigated and decided to use with Jonathan at home.

I met with the counsellor who advised me on how to implement the programme and I was very keen to begin work immediately. The programme was divided into sections that dealt with areas such as occupational therapy, speech therapy, physiotherapy and social skills. I decided that if this was going to replace school for Jonathan, I needed to do it properly. I set up a timetable that slotted in with Jonathan's morning sleep and separated the programme into sessions that I would apply for two hours in the morning and an hour in the afternoon, every school day.

I probably thought that because I was planning and managing the programme, Jonathan was going to comply with it. I spent many frustrating months trying to get his attention and cooperation. He would not participate in the physio exercises; he was very strong and would crawl away leaving me sitting on the floor. I pulled him back time and time again, and he mistook this for a game. Any efforts to do exercise therapy after that failed, unless I had another pair of hands to help me. As far as speech therapy was concerned, he absolutely refused to be part of it. I would do the 'ma-ma-ma-ma' and he would look at me as if I'd lost my mind. The occupational therapy consisted, at that stage, of attempting to bang two blocks together or putting shapes into shape slots which were invariably flung across the room like missiles. Because Jonathan loved music so much, I did part of the morning session to the accompaniment of a nursery rhyme music tape. He normally cooperated for a while, clapping at the appropriate time and listening intently to his 'teapot' or 'incy wincy spider' favourites. I normally did the music segment in the middle of the session so as to get him back on track and put him in the mood for the rest of the session. His only redeeming feature was the sparkle in his eyes while the music was playing. He had the most adorable little face and an endearing nature, which disguised a will of iron.

Half the year had gone and I had made very little progress with Jonathan. His mealtimes were still a bun fight and we had not advanced very far in the programme. I started dreading each day, knowing I was going to be pulling my hair out within ten minutes. Jonathan has always been very certain about what he will and won't do, and if he says 'no', it generally means just that. It served me right. I had too often pointed fingers at other people's children for not being controllable and here I was with a child who was calling the shots at every turn. My mother had high behavioural expectations and standards for her children and it was very hard to accept that Jonathan was never going to conform. He just didn't have the logic to understand expectations and standards, but has learnt appropriate behaviour by example and training.

After realising how little I had achieved with Jonathan in six months, I decided I was not using the correct teaching format for him. I did away with the structured sessions and started incorporating the therapy into our normal day. When I had him on the changing table to change his nappy, I would sing the songs and do the actions that accompanied them. I did some of the exercises too because he could not wriggle away from me. If he was making louder than usual noises as he crawled around the house at top speed, I would take it as a sign that it was time for me to run after him to do the 'da-da-da-da' routine. He would sometimes respond with a babbling sound. His speech was very delayed and it was only when he was very much older that he could copy a few familiar and common sounds. There was no set time or place to work with Jonathan so if I heard him and Graeme playing with something, I would ask Graeme to show him how to bang things together, which requires motor skills at that mental age.

Graeme was as good as ever with Jonathan and changing the structure of the programme allowed him and Barry to become more involved. I used to hear Barry changing Jonathan, doing all the things he'd heard me do. Graeme often tried the exercises with Jonathan when they crawled around together and any of Jonathan's new developments were attributed to his and Barry's efforts. They were so proud when Jonathan mastered something new and showed it off as 'Look what I've taught Jonathan to do'. Barry's day always started with a smile when he heard Jonathan calling from his cot. He would wake up and prepare the early morning bottle and make tea for the rest of us, and I'd hear him chatting away to Jonathan. The relief was indescribable! Barry had come full circle: Jonathan was his reason for getting up in the mornings and one of his reasons for living.

Unfortunately, my health problems persisted and I continued, as I had since Jonathan's birth and long before, to suffer from endless headaches. If ever I question what has happened to me in my life, I ask 'Why the headaches?' It would have been so much easier over the last twenty years to lead a normal life, or as normal as our household gets, without them. I am resigned to the fact that it is unlikely that they will disappear, despite being number one on my wish list of things to go.

Estelle was no longer visiting us and I hoped it was because she could see that I was coping, with Barry's full support and assistance. Although Jonathan was exceptionally hard work, he brought so much happiness and laughter to our home. What I remember most about this stage was how feeding time turned from a nightmare into a time of family fun. I didn't get Jonathan's feeding under control in the year I had him at home, but I managed to make trying a lot more pleasant. There were a lot of songs sung, animal sounds and general cavorting while he was perched in his feeding chair in the kitchen. If we caught him by surprise while he was wrapped up in the fun, occasionally a spoonful of food would go down by mistake. Although many children of his age with Down syndrome were feeding themselves, Jonathan was not yet able to grip anything for any length of time and his coordination was not good enough to guide the spoon to his mouth. If he were able to guide food anywhere, however, I'm sure it wouldn't have been to his mouth.

Jonathan would crawl down the passage at the speed of light, and you could hear the hurricane approaching, as he gave himself carpet burns on his knees as he went. His knees and hands were quite calloused from crawling at that speed and many of his sleepsuits had holes in the knees. It was quite difficult to take him out when he was that age, because he didn't want to stay in the pushchair for long and once he was out, he was all over the place. If he had been able to walk, one could at least have gripped his hand to keep him next to one. You might be thinking 'What do you mean, he didn't want to stay in the pushchair?' This is a question I would have asked before I had Jonathan, wondering what had become of parental control. But there was no logic or understanding of consequences. There was no punishment that taught him not to do it again. He didn't comprehend a gruff tone of voice to be one of displeasure. He was like a wind-up toy that powered full steam ahead until he wound down at night, the night's rest giving him his rewind.

Jonathan's night's rest was never very long. Hyperactive children generally do not sleep for long. For us, who were coping with Jonathan and trying to lead some sort of life ourselves, the nights felt five minutes long. Towards exam time I was working at night and getting up early in the mornings to study, with Barry supporting and encouraging me every step of the way.

Graeme had started school and thrilled us with his progress. I remember him practising his reading with Jonathan and really believing that Jonathan was benefiting from the stories of Rover the dog. If Jonathan stopped crawling for one second, it was taken as a sign that he was interested in what Graeme was reading, not that he just loved to be where his brother was. He would often crawl at full tilt towards Graeme and plant himself squarely on his lap and stay there for as long as he ever stayed anywhere, ten seconds, while Graeme continued reading with his book at arm's length above Jonathan's head. The gift I have been given, while coping with a very active existence, is to see Graeme and Jonathan together. It is an indescribable bond. If brothers could be made to order, Graeme would have been custom-built. All parents are naturally proud of their children, but the sensitivity and devotion he displayed was truly remarkable for his age.

I tried very hard to help Jonathan develop in every way that year. Over and above using the early intervention principles, I would regularly take him to the zoo to show him the animals, read to him and play in sand or water for tactile development. Nothing was of great interest to Jonathan at that age and I sometimes thought the only answer would be to clamp his head in a vice to get his attention so that I could show him new things. You know what they say about taking a horse to water, well, I'm sure that even with his head clamped, Jonathan would have refused to make eye contact.

The only success I had in teaching Jonathan anything was to do it via music. Music made him stop and listen and even exercises to music started working. It thrilled us all when we sang, 'This is the way we wash our face, wash our face, wash our face' and Jonathan started doing the face washing action with his hands. It soon turned to, 'This is the way we brush our teeth', 'clap our hands' or 'stamp our feet', and

Jonathan could do it all. You would have to have seen the proud look on Jonathan's face while he was doing his repertoire to know how we felt. We never tired of asking him to do it again and he never tired of doing it. Every time we saw the family, he would show off what he could do, to their absolute delight. His actions and clapping may not seem very important now, but they represented enormous developmental progress. He could hear, see, mimic and concentrate, things parents of genetically normal children usually take for granted.

Chapter 15

Jonathan's year at home was over and it was time for him to go back to school. Because it was a familiar place to him and because he was well at the time, he slotted back into the routine better than I anticipated. I had become used to having him with me, but the freedom it gave me for five hours every day was very welcome.

Jonathan's going back to school was hard for me, something I hadn't expected. The children at the school had grown and developed in the year that he'd been away and it was patently clear to me that the children with Down syndrome of Jonathan's age were functioning at a much higher level than he was. Most were walking and talking and they were all much more cooperative and easier to cope with than Jonathan was. I think it was at that point that I realised that Jonathan was not the same as the other children with Down syndrome. I admit I had trouble coming to terms with that. I had never been one of those competitive mothers who stood on the sidelines at Graeme's school sports screaming 'Go, go, go' and demanding he bring out the killer instinct. This was different, though; it was like having to accept all over again. Why couldn't Jonathan have just been like all the others?

116

It was then that I first acknowledged that Down syndrome comes in varying degrees. I had always thought that Down syndrome was Down syndrome and the effort you put into the child's training and development explained the difference in individual ability. This was not saying very much about my efforts. To make it worse, something happened that set me back for some time. Soon after Jonathan was back at school, the mothers were invited to watch a day of classroom activities to see what their children were achieving. Because of the children's ages and the fact that many of them were not cooperative when their families were around, some of us gathered outside the classroom to peep through the window to see them in action. It was upsetting for the parents of the more disabled children, but for the parents of the brighter ones it must have been a great thrill. I was standing next to a mother who I had come to know and like, and whose daughter with Down syndrome was one of the very able children in the class. She turned to me while looking at the activities in the classroom and said, 'Have you just left Jonathan in his cot for the last few years? Why has he not developed?' I think that was the cruellest thing anyone has ever said to me. I don't remember how I responded, but the remark wounded me, particularly as this little boy and his development were first and foremost in all our lives.

Jonathan had a very dedicated teacher that year and she tried very hard to include him in all the activities. He must have been hard work in a classroom because he never sat still. One of the classroom assistants, Milly, took him under her wing and seemed to care about him a great deal. It often happened that a teacher or assistant would form an attachment to him. Jonathan was hyperactive, exhausting, uncooperative and disinterested, but he was, and still is, a very affectionate child who showers love on the people who care about him. He made a dash for Milly each morning when we got to school and sometimes when I was doing committee work at the school, I'd notice her putting him on the swings or carrying him around with her. I have the highest regard for the people who choose this career.

At about that time we moved into a new house. We had decided that the kitchen needed to be remodelled, so we started renovations the day we moved in. There was chaos over the next few days with workmen coming and going from our property. Barry and I were standing in the kitchen talking to the builder one afternoon when a man in a suit walked in, carrying Jonathan. 'I saw him crawl into the middle of the road and he just sat there,' he said. He had been driving home from work and had come across this unusual sight, pulled over and brought Jonathan home. His words echoed in my mind for a long time and I was so stunned that I'm not sure I even thanked him properly. We had only taken our eyes off Jonathan for a second, but the builder had left the gate open and he took the gap.

That incident was the start of recurring nightmares I had about Jonathan's safety. I would often dream about him getting out of our property and crawling down the street onto someone else's. I would wake up in a sweat after dreaming that I'd run up and down the street, calling his name, not knowing where to look for him, worried that the homes might have unprotected swimming pools. I think the dreams represented the fears I had about Jonathan's safety and only over the last few years have I been able to let them go.

The nightmares had included water because Jonathan loved

swimming so much. I knew that if he came across water, he would probably crawl right into it, not knowing that it was his life jacket that normally kept him afloat. I have a clear picture in my mind of Jonathan with his striped life jacket on, being thrown into the pool and bobbing up gasping for breath and laughing at the same time. His love of water was a major concern until he could swim unaided, which was when he was about five years old.

Graeme would occasionally have friends over in the afternoons and they would all swim together. I have never seen Graeme behave differently towards Jonathan under any circumstances, not even when his friends were there. His friends always knew that Jonathan would be around when they were visiting Graeme. It may have put some of them off but those are probably the sort of friends that Graeme would not have chosen to keep anyway. I often tried to keep Jonathan away from Graeme thinking he would appreciate privacy with his friends but he would come looking for Jonathan, wondering where he was and take him back with him. The day a disabled child is born, so many lives are changed forever. When you look into the face of imperfection every day and really like what you see, it must change the perception you have of yourself and others. I think Graeme felt strong and comfortable with a commitment to teach and protect, which is probably why he has grown up to be a kind and responsible person.

Barry remained deeply committed to Jonathan. He travelled away on business from time to time and although Jonathan could not speak, Barry always wanted to talk to him when he phoned home. I would hold the phone to Jonathan's ear while Barry called his name and talked to him. Jonathan would stop, listen, recognise and look around to find his dad. He could not understand hearing Barry's voice without seeing him. His arms would flap in excitement and he would worm his way out of my arms and crawl like lightning to the door in the hope that Barry would walk through it. It was a ritual when Barry came home after a hard day's work each day that he would kiss both children and Graeme would hop around him in excitement while Barry flung Jonathan up in the air. The only word Jonathan had learnt to say was 'more' and he used it all the time. The shouting and excitement went on for ages until eventually Barry would retrieve his jacket and briefcase left in the doorway.

I am not certain when Graeme first came to understand the reality of Jonathan's disability. It was hard to tell when the realisation took place. Although I'm certain that Graeme knew that Jonathan was vulnerable almost from the moment he first saw him, and we never hid any facts from him, there must have been a time when he realised the seriousness of his brother's disability. If Graeme had treated his brother differently as a result of his disability, we would have been able to pinpoint when it was that he grasped that his brother was different. Because Graeme was three and a half years older than Jonathan, and Jonathan's behaviour was so babylike for so long, I don't suppose he would have had to think about it until he was about six years old. We talked about Down syndrome a lot at home but how do you explain to a small child how it manifests or what it actually means? He must have been able to think fairly abstractly to make a realistic assessment about his brother, compared to other children of Jonathan's age. I've often thought that it must have been when he was about eleven years old that Graeme assimilated all he had seen in his own home and compared it to what he had seen in other people's homes. Only then could he have made a judgement on the differences and long-term aspect of Jonathan's condition. While he was dealing with all this, all we saw was the same commitment and interest he had always shown towards Jonathan. We noticed that Graeme had learnt to adjust his conversation with Jonathan to be on the same wavelength as him. They had a type of language between them that they both understood. Barry and I understood it too but I'm not sure many others would have. Speech therapists would probably say that it could have been detrimental to a child's verbal development to converse in a language that would ultimately need to be altered for everyone else to understand. There again, judgements should be reserved when the child has a severe verbal problem. It was that or nothing. He doesn't say things like 'uppy' anymore and just as well, because he'd be better equipped to carry us around on his hip now that he's eighteen years old!

When Jonathan was about three, I took out some books and a few research papers on Down syndrome from the university library. I had bought and read several books on the subject at the time of Jonathan's birth but it was three years later and it amazed me how the information looked so different. Perhaps it was because I was able to relate to it better, having had three years of contact with Jonathan, or maybe I was relating the information to my work and not subjectively to my son. It's also a possibility that my true acceptance of Jonathan had made the information a lot less threatening. There is just so much you can learn about Down syndrome and a lot of the information is not really what parents need. All sorts of statistics are given regarding visual problems, heart problems and lung problems, to name just three. It can be upsetting because you don't know in the early stages which, if any, of these conditions will affect your child and you imagine that he will have all the possible symptoms described. The books are only a guideline to what may happen, and what has happened to some people in the past and should not be seen as a prediction of what the future may hold for anyone else. I feel the same way about this book; it is merely a story about a boy called Jonathan, his many challenges, and the cohesive impact he has had on our family. At no time would I suggest that other children with Down syndrome will be like him in any way, or even have similar problems. I also hope that his story will provide an insight into the joys and tragedies, the highs and lows, and the ecstasy and despair that rearing a child with a disability entails.

Jonathan was now four years old. He continued to contract pneumonia and I had started taking him to the provincial hospital because it was often difficult to get a private doctor to see him at night. It unnerved me when Jonathan turned blue and it took so long to track down our doctor to have him admitted to the hospital. I knew Jonathan's trick of springing illness on us and I felt better about taking him directly to the provincial hospital. Today we take him to any emergency room of the local private hospitals, but in those days the private hospitals did not offer that service.

One night he was battling to breathe and I raced him to the hospital, leaving Barry at home with Graeme. He was blue by the time we arrived and was taken straight through for X-rays to confirm that he had pneumonia. He was sent up to the ward and put into an oxygen tent where they had to tie him down to get an antibiotic drip into his veins. Once all the panic and fuss was over and Jonathan had gone to sleep, after exhausting himself by fighting anyone who came near him, I sat and watched him feeling greatly relieved. A nursing sister came to talk to me and mentioned that there was another child with Down syndrome in the ward. I knew he was there because I had visited him a few days before and had already popped my head in the door while Jonathan was being attended to. It was a friend's child, Johan, a little boy slightly younger than Jonathan. He had been diagnosed with leukaemia and was undergoing chemotherapy. My friend, Leona, sat with him for the six weeks it took before he died. I have an enduring memory of her sitting with him on her lap in the oxygen tent, clinging to him until the end. I felt so sad and so fortunate at the same time.

Leona and I had organised a Down syndrome Baby Competition for the Down Syndrome Association. It was held at the Sunshine Centre and a television personality was involved in choosing a winner from every age group and finally the overall winner. It was announced at the function that one of the organisers was unable to attend because her child had been taken ill. That was how I heard about Johan for the first time. I accepted Leona's basket of flowers on her behalf, the association's thanks for her hard work, and took it to her in the hospital.

Jonathan and Graeme had a spate of childhood illnesses later that year. If it wasn't chickenpox, it was German measles or scarlet fever. It seemed one or both of them were up at night for months on end, either throwing up or with high fevers. When one set of spots disappeared, another took its place. Childhood illnesses are inevitable and I suppose having them concentrated in a few months lets you off the hook for a few years.

Chapter 16

Jonathan whizzed around on all fours until he one day decided to stand up and walk. He had been pulling himself up on anything, often not gauging that it was not strong enough to hold his weight. He was four years old and very heavy to carry around, particularly up the steep slope at the Sunshine Centre. He had been walking and holding on to the furniture for some time so it didn't come as a surprise to us that he was ready to take his first steps, because he had been midway between walking and crawling for a while. He'd try to take a few steps, collapse to his knees because crawling was so easy for him, and then stand up and try again.

I would like to say that there was great pomp and ceremony the day Jonathan took his first steps, but I'm afraid the walking just sort of evolved. He went from crawling to walking to running in no time at all and that is when our lives felt as if the fast forward button had been turned on and everything was happening at top speed. Speed and Jonathan's lack of ability to understand safety were a major problem. He was a loose cannon! He had absolutely no idea that he could bump into things and that they could bump into him. He just surged ahead as if forward and fast were the only words he knew. He never looked back and as a result didn't learn from consequences and totally ignored verbal instructions or warnings. It was as though he could only do one thing at a time and that was running. Running and listening did not go together – multitasking was not in his repertoire. It took me a long time to figure that out, but I continued to shout at him, if only for the purpose of releasing my own pent up frustration. There is nothing worse than seeing your child moving towards something potentially dangerous and having no power to stop him.

One would think that Jonathan's ability to walk would have been a big relief but it in fact made life a great deal harder. It was often safer to hold him on my hip than to let him go. The minute he was free he would dash away and head nowhere in particular, but always forwards. A lot of people saw it as him trying to run away, but I don't think he could assess that he was here and wanted to be there; he just ran for the sake of moving – that's what hyperactive children do. Trying to take him to a public place was a nightmare unless he was strapped into a pushchair. He would pull away and disappear within seconds. In a supermarket one afternoon, he was sitting in the child's seat in the front of the supermarket trolley and verbally laying down the law. He was not only making a noise and had everyone staring, but was trying to climb out of the trolley from time to time and grabbing things as we walked down the aisles. He was behaving very badly and I was losing my patience, probably as a result of exhaustion and embarrassment. I pulled up to a checkout point and waited behind a woman who was unloading her trolley. Jonathan started pulling items off the checkout shelves. I had had enough by then and gave him a smart smack on the back of the hand and told him he wouldn't come shopping with me again. The woman ahead of us could not see Jonathan because he was facing the other way and she looked in my general direction and said indignantly, 'I can't stand to hear mothers getting impatient with their children in supermarkets.' I know she hadn't finished what she was going to say to me but I wasn't giving her the chance. I was enraged and said without thinking, 'Well, you bloody well take him home with you then!' With that Jonathan turned to see what the fuss was about and she saw his face for the first time. It made me squirm to see her embarrassment and I think we both learnt something from that. She learnt not to interfere in other people's business and I learnt to speak more quietly to Jonathan when I was reprimanding him in public.

In the vertical position, Jonathan could see things differently. Countertops and tabletops were within his reach and he had the most compelling desire to scoop everything on them onto the floor. I have never understood it, but I'm sure developmental psychologists would have an explanation. Another thing he would do was push things over. The plastic outdoor tables at school were flipped over, irrespective of what was on them and every chair in our house was pushed onto its side at every opportunity. If Jonathan saw a container of small toys like blocks or Lego, he would immediately tip it upside down, scattering them everywhere and then move onto the next thing he could destroy. He was rapidly losing popularity at home and at school.

While he was creating havoc, he was a happy and secure little boy. He would hold my face between his two rough little hands and look at me adoringly before he planted a kiss on my mouth. It gave the word 'gobsmacked' a new meaning! He didn't know much about a lot of things, but he knew all about love. He was very affectionate and had a way of making any hardship worth it.

I tried everything I could think of to punish or dissuade his wild non-conforming behaviour. I took out books from the university library on parental guidance and control strategies, but they didn't mention anything about a child who was like a drumming bunny with a battery that couldn't be removed and lasted forever. His behaviour was automatic. The books talked about reasoning with the child and creating incentives, but that was clearly for a child with an intact left brain. Reasoning with Jonathan at four years old was as effective as giving him a large steak and asking him to swallow it – he couldn't do it.

Because he was uncharacteristically tall for his age, he could reach door handles, so closed doors no longer contained him. He had become obsessed with lights and could also reach the light switches. He would turn all the lights on in the house and I'd turn them all off and this could go on a few times during the day unless I followed him around and stopped him doing it in the first place. He was doing it at school too. The computers in the office switched off one day and the lights went out. Apparently it was usual, under the circumstances, for the staff to come rushing out asking after Jonathan's whereabouts, knowing that it could only be his handiwork. He had climbed on top of the lockers to reach the mains switch before scuttling down and returning to his classroom without anyone noticing. The first time this happened, the staff had been confused as to why the school power was on, but the office power was off. They did what they thought most appropriate and asked Jonathan to turn

127

the lights back on and they watched him clamber up onto the lockers and stand on his tiptoes to reach the switch. They hadn't realised that it was the mains switch for the office before Jonathan pointed it out to them.

It became increasingly difficult and exhausting to take Jonathan to other people's homes. Unless you were trailing behind him to see where he was going he disappeared into a household that felt like a maze when it came to looking for him. Socialising away from home became a nightmare and was not the leisure activity it was intended to be. As a result, we started inviting people to our home more often than we accepted invitations to go out. At least we knew, while we were enjoying our friends' company, that Jonathan was safe and not able to get out of the grounds, which was something we were never sure of elsewhere. It happened more than once that while in other people's homes, he would push the panic button, sounding a deafening siren and summoning the security service. He also activated a Mace spray attached to a bunch of keys in someone's home, causing everyone to dash for fresh air, choking and gasping for breath. It was kinder for us all to stay at home until he learnt that actions had consequences, which, of course, he eventually did.

Mealtimes became calmer and we were making good progress in getting Jonathan to feed himself. It was an extremely messy business because he was still only eating mashed food and didn't have good control over a spoon. School and home were synchronising expectations, so we were all trying to achieve the same goal. I remember Jonathan sitting in his high chair feeding himself, with food all over his face and all over the floor around his chair. He was always happy and because mealtimes had, out of necessity, become playtime, Jonathan always pulled out all the tricks while he was in his chair. He would babble, copy animal sounds and laugh heartily, food flying everywhere and pride written all over his face. It was no wonder: he had learnt to hold a spoon and feed himself, make animal sounds and enjoy mealtimes. He had everything to be proud of.

He loved sitting in his high chair but he was close to five years old and becoming a bit too big for it. It was the kind of chair that could be adjusted to be a low chair that looked like a racing car when it was tipped over. He sat in that chair to eat for many years; it had seen many traumatic times and by the time it was turned into a chariot, it had truly been 'broken in'.

It was time to begin toilet training now that Jonathan was running around. It was hard to find nappies to fit him and he was often tripped up by one that had collapsed around his ankles. The nappy system wasn't designed for big and busy boys. Because I could no longer get disposable nappies in his size, I resorted to towelling nappies and nappy pins. It was a long process of getting him to understand and act on the urge to use the toilet. It went on for about a year and towards the end of that time he was wearing training pants during the day and a nappy at night. Success was achieved by trying to anticipate the need to go to the toilet. I put him on the toilet every couple of hours during the day, and at night I would make sure he'd used the toilet before bedtime. We would also wake him up and sit him on the toilet before we went to bed at around midnight. When I say 'wake him', I don't believe he ever woke up. He had started to talk towards the end of the toilet training and was then six years old.

A particularly hilarious interlude in his toilet training came when we went to an internationally renowned resort for the boys to enjoy a day of swimming in the electronic wave pool that had recently been opened. When it was time to go home, Jonathan and I were sitting on a bench outside the changing rooms waiting for Barry and Graeme who were taking longer to dress than we had. A man stopped near us to open his locker. He had been swimming and had a wet patch on the front of his swimming trunks. Jonathan leapt out of his seat and dashed towards him, prodding him hard in the crotch and instructing him loudly: 'Wee-wee in the toilet!' Horrified, I rushed towards Jonathan, grabbed him by the hand and marched him away without looking back at the man's reaction.

Jonathan's speech improved every day. He could say 'Mommy', 'Daddy', 'Game' and 'Ganny'. 'Game' was his brother's name and 'Ganny' was my mother. Although his verbal communication was limited, he could make himself very well understood. He has a sort of sixth sense about whether the person he is communicating with has understood him. If he believes that you have not grasped what he has said, he rephrases it by giving you a second clue and more often than not, enough to piece together what he is driving at. Before I ever handed anything to Jonathan I would hesitate, only giving it to him when he said 'thank you' and that now comes as second nature to him.

His basis for learning has been mimicry rather than logic, and he has learnt good manners and the way to conduct himself by example, not from understanding that it is the right thing to do. This mimicry reveals itself every day, and it's quite disconcerting when it is done in my exact tone of voice and with my mannerisms, highlighting my involvement in the moulding of this vulnerable human being. One day he was talking on his imaginary cell phone in the car on the way home from school, his index finger serving as the aerial. He often uses this form of communication with people he cares about and it always fascinates me that he's quiet for an appropriate length of time so that the imaginary recipient can reply. He was in the middle of talking to Cathy, my sister, when I had a coughing spell. He put his other hand over the imaginary mouthpiece and looked daggers at me, saying, 'I'm on the phone!' Yes, I have said that before and he did learn that tone from me. He then went back to Cath and said, 'Sorry, Caf, it's a bad dream!' and carried on with his conversation with her. One must understand that he has absolutely no concept of what a bad dream is. That is mimicry at its finest. I have often had a very good reason for saying 'This is a nightmare' but I don't think I ever have. He might have heard his school friends talking about it. He may have had nightmares, we all do, but I don't think we could ever explain the concept to him. I think his sunny, happy face has always mimicked the love he has received from our family, our friends and us. For instance, he once looked adoringly at me, holding my face in his chapped, horny little hands. I thought he was going to say something profound from the way he was looking at me. He did. He said, 'You sweet boy!'

Chapter 17

You probably have visions of Jonathan being a small, scrawny and underfed child. He was, in fact, robust and almost podgy until he was four. Once he started walking and running, he lost some of his podginess, as children of that age often do. When I look at photographs taken of him for the baby competition, I find it amazing that he looked so healthy when we had so much trouble getting food down his throat. Sustenance had come mainly from his porridge-thickened milk.

He had matured physically and although he was like a baby in many ways, he mastered many things quickly. We put a jungle gym in the garden because he seemed to love the one at school. The first few weeks were a nail-biting experience, but after that he amazed us with his ability to climb and hold on. It was surprising that he never fell off because he was clumsy, uncoordinated and had very little sense of danger.

He was still sleeping in a cot but it was getting a little small for him. The problem with putting him in a bed was that he would climb out in the middle of the night and skulk around the house. We stepped up our night vigil because he was trying to do new things, which we were always pleased about, but one of them was taking a milk bottle out of the fridge and letting it slip from his grasp. In those days we still had milk delivered in glass bottles.

Jonathan would wake after his afternoon nap and play the game of stripping his bedding and throwing it out of the cot onto the floor, until he was standing on the springs of the cot, playing trampoline with the mattress overboard. The rule with Jonathan was that if there was quiet in the house, it meant he was either asleep or up to no good. It was a rule that worked every time. When he finally got too big for the cot, he merely climbed over the side of it, making the purpose of it pointless. We put him in a bed and would occasionally hear a thud in the middle of the night when he fell out. On a few occasions we found him curled up on the floor fast asleep when he had fallen out of bed and just stayed there.

Swimming is one of Jonathan's passions and he has always loved the water. It gave him great pleasure to throw things over the pool fence into the water. Books, shoes, toys, fruit, anything! I'm not sure if it was anything to do with the water, or if it was the fence that created the challenge for him. I think he may have viewed it as a goal scored if whatever he was throwing went over and a further point if it landed in the water. I went with my friend Margie, her two girls and Graeme and Jonathan to the zoo one afternoon. Jonathan was still in his pushchair and we had whizzed him around, showing him all the animals and he had shown off all he knew about animal sounds. We got to the seal enclosure and sat on the bench to watch them. The seals were on top form that day and we were all so interested in their antics that we didn't see Jonathan take off one of his shoes; all we saw was a shoe flying over the fence into the seal pond.

It was driving us all crazy that so many of our things ended up in the pool, including Graeme's schoolbooks. Don't think that I had a philosophical approach to it then. There was shouting, screaming, smacking and punishing going on all the time. The light switches were still a problem, all lights on, all lights off, then all lights on again. The cupboards he could reach were unpacked on a daily basis and unless my eyes were on him all the time, I would be faced with some form of chaos. I answered the phone one day and when I came back into the kitchen, I got the fright of my life because I could not make sense of the apparition before me. It was Jonathan coated from head to toe in cake flour.

I wasn't alone; the school was also having their fair share of problems. Jonathan decided one day to wash his hands in the basin, so he put the plug in and left the tap running, which flooded the ablution block. Because of the background I had come from, I never got used to having to take responsibility for my child's bad behaviour. I felt singled out as the mother of the troublemaker of the school and it looked like we were soft, weak parents, which we weren't. It was clear that Graeme was a well-adjusted, and well-behaved child but we really could not control Jonathan and it used to upset us when professionals suggested that we were over-protective or not firm enough with him. I was never soft and the same rules applied for Jonathan as they did for Graeme at the same mental age. There is little understanding unless you are involved first-hand in a situation like ours, that children like Jonathan have no capacity for logic and act on impulse or instinct. What appears to be naughty is actually just not knowing better. Without a database of life's experiences against which to compare your own behaviour, how can you tell what is right or wrong?

The only way to teach a person with no facility for logic is to train them. Training is different from teaching in that teaching entails getting someone to learn something by understanding it, while training is getting someone to an agreed standard of proficiency by practice and instruction. I believe Jonathan has been trained to be the wonderful boy he is today through ongoing practice and instruction. Everything Jonathan has achieved has been the result of being shown something and then practising it until he got it right. If he was not getting it right, it meant he had not practised it enough or needed more instruction. Being shown and then copying is a form of mimicry and I know that just about everything Jonathan does, he has copied from someone else. As he has grown older, though, he has been able to understand that his actions will have consequences and to learn from that. Because he learns by example, it has placed responsibility on the people around him to teach and mould him as they think beneficial. When he says 'That's nice', it could be my voice he's using, and when he lets off a loud hearty laugh just like Barry's, it is a reminder, however daunting, of the role we constantly play in his development.

When he was six years old Jonathan could operate our hi-fi set, our television and our video recorder. He had learnt by watching Graeme and it took him no time at all to master the use of the new hi-fi set Barry had bought. I remember wanting to play a CD and not knowing how to work the new equipment, so I called Jonathan and asked him to help me. He flicked the 'on' button and took the CD from me. He then opened the case and held the disk in the correct manner, not putting his fingers on any part of it that mattered. He pushed a button, which ejected the shuttle, and placed the CD on the disk holder marked number one. He pushed another button, which sucked the CD into the player and with a flick of a button, the CD was playing. He then adjusted the volume and went back to what he was doing before I called him. There was no conversation while he did it and no need for a fanfare when it was done, and the strange part was that I was not surprised. I had become used to what he was capable of and knew exactly what he could and couldn't do. While I knew he was capable of working this technical equipment, I also knew that if he could have lifted it, there was a distinct possibility that it could have ended up in the pool!

We had come to love Jonathan so dearly that we were able to overlook his shortcomings. We understood him and Down syndrome so well that we made allowances for the fact that a lot of his behaviour was beyond his control or understanding.

It is easy to judge children like Jonathan and to judge the way they are handled, because making comparisons is such a human failing. The comparison, in this case, is made using all that is known about genetically normal human functioning and applying it to a situation that is totally unrelated. The fundamental rule about comparison is that it should be like with like.

Despite the fact that we did not hold Jonathan accountable for his actions, we remained firm in our handling of him. This resulted in many a heel being dug in on both sides, but Barry and I were not going to become 'pushovers', no matter how much pressure Jonathan put on us. Consistency is paramount; without it the rules become confusing. Having consistent rules, however, did not mean that Jonathan was going to conform to them without testing them. It was only with time and endurance that the rules became entrenched.

We were battling to cope with the constant vigil required to keep Jonathan safe and this resulted in Barry and I arguing over whose turn it was on a Saturday afternoon to be on guard. I sometimes resented not having a quiet and peaceful life like my friends with children of the same age. There was no reading a book or taking a nap, as it was look and listen at all times. Hyperactive children require very little sleep, so there were no long sleeps during the day and wake-up time was early in our house because we could no longer keep Jonathan contained in his cot.

That year we put a security gate up in Jonathan's room. He usually woke up at around four thirty and either Barry or I would get up and give him some breakfast, make sure he'd gone to the toilet, then put him in his room with the gate closed and we would try to get another hour's sleep. He would play with his toys and hurl things around his room, not at all unhappy about being there. Because the door was never closed, he never felt cut off from us. It was a safe place to leave him and I viewed it as a giant playpen. It worked well until a friend visited one day, saw the gate and strongly voiced her opinion about my jailing tactics. It never felt like respite after that, because guilt had crept in and we stopped using the gate. One should try to resist being influenced by negative criticism because the parent usually knows best.

The days were long and the nights were short. Our home

was not a place of tranquillity, but we survived by caring really deeply for one another. Graeme was in the middle of the storm, but probably did not remember life in good weather. He was nine years old and wise beyond his years. He knew home as the chaotic but happy place it had become. I often wondered whether, when he visited his friends in their homes, he marvelled at the peacefulness.

Jonathan was much healthier between the ages of six and seven. He seemed to have outgrown his chest problem and visits to the hospital in the middle of the night became less frequent. He had had most of the childhood illnesses and his immune system seemed to have strengthened. The time to think about formal education or 'big school' had arrived.

Chapter 18

It was customary for the Sunshine Centre to see that the children ready for formal education were suitably placed in schools appropriate to their disability and it still works like that today. Formal education refers to the twelve years between the ages of approximately six and eighteen that a child is legally bound to attend school. Special education refers to the specially designed instruction that meets the unique or individual needs of an exceptional student, exceptional in this case meaning mentally disabled.

There are not many facilities near our home for special education, and there is a waiting list for students wanting to get into the special education schools, apart from class one. It was logistically a natural progression for the children living in the vicinity of the Sunshine Centre to move on to Casa Do Sol School for formal education. In the last year at the Sunshine Centre, Casa Do Sol assesses the children who will move on, and then accept or decline applications at that point. I had been told, unofficially, that the assessment had taken place and Jonathan had been accepted and would start school at Casa Do Sol in January of the following year. We were thrilled because it meant progress, but we were also sad to leave everything familiar behind. I had been involved with the parent association for a number of years and was starting to feel like a part of the establishment. We always knew that Jonathan would have to leave the Sunshine Centre when he was seven years old, but he looked so young to be starting school. Perhaps he didn't actually look young, but starting school is a milestone that comes with a clear and prescribed picture in all our minds. I think people have visions of a child of a certain height standing like a tin soldier in a uniform, grinning with some front teeth missing. That's the first day of school picture I have in my mind, anyway. Jonathan wasn't like that. Firstly, Casa Do Sol does not have a school uniform policy and secondly, Jonathan was immature, had all his front teeth and was physically a lot more active than any tin soldier.

The children at the Sunshine Centre were given a memorable farewell to celebrate their graduation. The photographs are a reminder of how much care was taken to make the occasion the milestone that it was. This was the end of an era and the beginning of another and we had no idea of what lay ahead.

I took Jonathan to Casa Do Sol for his first day of school with an open mind as to how they would cope with him. He looked so different to what you would expect a school child to look like and I could not picture Jonathan sitting at a desk like Graeme did on his first day at school. Many children had moved on from the Sunshine Centre, so there was an air of familiarity. I knew some of the teachers and parents and had met Joy, the headmistress, at previous functions, so it was not at all threatening.

I can truthfully say that the idea of Jonathan going to school for the first time, if he had not had Down syndrome, had not crossed my mind. I have never thought about milestones that might have been or related the milestones of my friends' children to Jonathan in any way. Margie's daughter Frances is a similar age to Jonathan and it probably would have been her that I would have compared him with, but I never did. It didn't strike me until a few years after Frances started high school, that it could have been Jonathan going into a different phase of his life. I am fortunate that comparing Jonathan was not an issue for me. I have known people with disabled children who have never overcome the disappointment of what might have been. Jonathan is so unique in every way that comparisons of any kind have never been possible. Maybe this is an indication of true and unconditional acceptance. The wish for him to be different, particularly more manageable, was there in the earlier years of his life but now that he was seven years old, he was never anything but Jonathan. We all accepted and loved him as he had been given to us, despite the fact that he regularly tipped our lives into total disarray. The love we felt for Jonathan was not out of pity or protection; it was a deep, meaningful love with no conditions.

Jonathan was still not aware of consequences, other than the ones that were reinforced with a fair amount of unpleasantness, and even then continual reinforcement was required. He was agile, despite the fact that he has always had an awkward gait, and could run away at quite a speed. I could never understand his need to dash off, heading nowhere and with no motive. I suppose he was just a hyperactive boy on the move. I have since come across a few other mentally disabled children who are the same, although it is quite unusual. With no agenda or intention, they run as fast as they can in an unpredictable direction. One actually

141

needed ten hands to cope with Jonathan, not one. I used to get him out of the car and trap him against the door while I coped with locking it and gathering my handbag. I would physically have to pin him to the side of the car so that he couldn't get away. He came to expect it and never fought me and today he gets out of the car and stands right up next to the door until I tell him where we are going and reassure him that it is fine to move away. I don't think he has respect for the danger involved in those situations, but he's come to respect that there are rules related to them.

Jonathan had no need for company when he was seven years old. He did not interact with other children, but rather learnt by their behaviour. He did not play games with them, but enjoyed watching them play with each other. As a result, he was not a troublemaker when it came to sharing things with others, but he was disruptive because he was permanently on the move. It must have been very difficult in the classroom, given the fact that the other seven children in his class had their own problems.

I expected Jonathan to look vulnerable and unsure on his first day of school, but he didn't. Instead I felt vulnerable and unsure, as his mother. I picked him up at noon, expecting to get reports of how he'd 'toed the line' and was now a big schoolboy who needed to fit in. You often hear people say, 'Well, school will sort him out.' I had thought this was going to be the turning point in our lives. Instead I was met by a teacher who looked as if she'd gone the full ten rounds in a boxing ring and lost. She looked exhausted. I heard about Jonathan getting away a few times and having to be dragged back, trapping his foot under the rocking equipment and refusing to eat. 'More of the same,' I thought and took him home. Every day of that first week was the same. I would get to the school to fetch him and was told of countless misdemeanours. The biggest problem was that the gates of the school were never closed and it faced a very busy road, close to a busy intersection. I never understood why the gates were left open when the school was a facility for children who did not function normally. When I asked I was told that the school was a place of learning, not of care. The subsequent rise in crime has now led to the gates being permanently locked, serving not only to keep the nasty elements out, but also the roving children in.

I am now often very proud of Jonathan's behaviour and it seems a long time ago that his behaviour and inability to understand simple social rules embarrassed me. I do think it was harder for me than it would have been if I had a different personality. I have always been so aware of people around me, and I know that this concern for others in relation to our children's behaviour is a family trait because I have seen it in my own brothers and sisters. It has its benefits because it often results in well-behaved children and respect for others, but it has been very hard for me and something Barry has found difficult to understand. I often wish I had the same attitude to Jonathan's behaviour as Barry does. He has been able to allow Jonathan freedom, irrespective of who is watching. He becomes oblivious to others in his interaction with Jonathan, irrespective of the circumstances. I, on the other hand, see it as a personal weakness if I cannot control my child. I am also far more sensitive than Barry about Jonathan behaving in a way that makes him look silly. There is for me a fine line between being cute and looking foolish. Barry just doesn't see it. I think the pride he feels for his son overrides any possibility of foolishness. Barry has allowed

Jonathan to take centre stage and sing the national anthem in a crowded shopping centre, with the supermarket packers dancing in appreciation, while I would sooner die. You have to see the look on Barry's face to know the deep pride I'm referring to. It shows that there is not a right or wrong way to show acceptance, only different ways. Barry would never let Jonathan lose his dignity, but loves others to enjoy Jonathan as he does, while Graeme falls somewhere between us. I was expecting him to go through a time of embarrassment when he was a teenager, but he never did.

The first big mistake Jonathan made at Casa Do Sol was to run out of the gate during his second week. Joy, the headmistress, saw him go and ran after him. Joy was not a young woman and had to charge down the street after a boy who had no road sense and no particular plan of action. She told me he kept looking back at her and laughing, as if it was a game of catch. The danger posed by the busy intersection was certainly of great concern to her. Along with her personal frustration and irritation, the black mark in his file must have been like an inkblot.

I was recently reminded of an incident I had all but forgotten. One day I was called to the school because Jonathan had gone missing. I was told that the police had been called and the entire school was scouring the grounds for a boy who was incapable of hiding quietly. He was found asleep in the sun on the back seat of one of the teachers' cars in the carpark. Now we know that a car or a bus is where you look first for Jonathan, but in those early days we still had to learn that.

He continued to be uncooperative and caused problems in the classroom. Joy had spoken to me a few times about the difficulties they were having so I was aware that there was a problem, but I did not know how serious it was.

The final 'nail in the coffin' came with the bus incident. Barry was on leave and had undertaken to fetch Jonathan from school. When he was a couple of blocks away from the school, he was flabbergasted to see the Casa Do Sol bus come down the road, with Jonathan sitting at the window. Barry did a U-turn, flagged the bus down and explained to the driver that his child should not have been on the bus, took him off and took him home. Barry did not phone the school when he got home to tell them what had happened, because he presumed that the school didn't realise that Jonathan was on the bus in the first place. After the bus had left the school, Jonathan was missed and the school thought he'd got out of the grounds. Panic set in. It was before the days of cellphones, so they had to wait for Barry to arrive home to tell him that Jonathan was gone. 'But I've got him,' Barry said. The inkblot now covered most of Jonathan's file and obliterated the progress of the first seven years of his life. It blotted out that he'd passed the test at the Sunshine Centre to go to big school. The only part it wasn't hiding was that Jonathan was a danger to himself.

I knew immediately that this incident was not going to go down well at the school, never dreaming that it would go down quite as badly as it did. I was expecting Joy to speak to me about it after the weekend and I was right. I was asked to see her and she explained that the risks involved in keeping Jonathan at Casa Do Sol were far too great. She had contacted the Sunshine Centre and they had decided that Jonathan should go back to their safe confines while a meeting was set up for us to go and see Tara again. Jonathan could not stay at the Sunshine Centre because of his age, but since the Sunshine Centre undertakes to place children who leave them, I'm sure they saw it as a commitment to do so until a solution had been found.

Joy went on to say that it was her personal belief, with all her years of experience, that the kind of disability Jonathan had would be better managed in a boarding school. It was her opinion that no normal household could cope with the demands he would place on us and accurately said that our lives were being turned into a game of cat and mouse. Barry had come with me to that meeting and we left her office and fetched Jonathan and went home. It felt like the end of the line and the thought of Tara again was more than a little defeating.

This was going to be a time of change, and was the most distressing time of my life. I needed to accept, adapt and dust myself off for new beginnings far more often than the average person does in a lifetime, but nothing was as hard as this because of the awful feeling of regression.

Chapter 19

Walking up the hill to the Sunshine Centre felt comforting and Jonathan, who has always thrived on routine, was also comforted. He had a loyal following in some of the staff and they again took up their positions in keeping a watchful eye on him, while at the same time showing him some special care. It was a relief to be back and to be able to leave him in a place where I knew he was safe. Although we had been battling to cope with Jonathan at home for some time, we had considered life as normal as it was going to get before the big school debacle raised its ugly head. It felt as if we were coping, but perhaps there would have been a limit as to how long we could have endured the responsibilities placed on us as a family.

The social worker at the Sunshine Centre called me into her office on Jonathan's first day back to discuss the situation. She had set up a meeting with Tara, with a view to suggesting behaviour modification for him before he was placed at another school (hopefully one with a better security policy). I now know that the advice the professionals gave us was out of concern for us and a better arrangement for the family, but I was outraged at the time. Perhaps deeply hurt is more accurate. Everyone was suggesting boarding school. The idea of sending Jonathan away had never occurred to us before and we were feeling traumatised. I suppose one always needs to vent anger on others when painful things happen that are beyond one's control. I think the pain I felt was somehow connected to the fact that I had grown to consider everyone at the Sunshine Centre, and anyone connected to mental disability in any way, as an extension of my family. It felt as though Jonathan had been rejected and belonged nowhere. It was a reinforcement of my feeling that he was not the same as the other children with Down syndrome and that made me sad, hurt and also extremely angry.

The appointment at Tara was made for a few weeks later, so we all settled back into relative quiet while we waited, with dread, to see where this would lead us.

The day of our appointment arrived. We took Jonathan along at the time and place the social worker had arranged and were sent to a different place at Tara than on our previous visit. A new facility had been created for the purpose of dealing with children with behavioural disorders. The little building was brightly painted and welcoming, and the staff, being the supportive facility it was, were receptive and friendly. Crossing the lawn towards the building, I had to stop and compose myself, wipe my eyes, blow my nose and then try and keep up with Barry who was holding Jonathan's hand and was being dragged along as if on a leash.

We were given a cup of coffee and Jonathan was taken care of by a few staff members whose job it was to do just that. He had them running, but because of the nature of the facility they must have come across children like Jonathan all the time. We were seated in an open-plan room that was set up for about ten people. While we waited for all the staff to arrive, we saw Jonathan bouncing off the walls and tipping things over as he went. A plastic table set up with games on it was tipped upside down and what was previously on the table was being hurled around. I decided that I would not look at what was going on. It was hard for me to consider it not to be my business, but I forced myself. The staff members had started arriving and there wasn't one we recognised from our last visit. When everyone was present, Barry and I were introduced to the team, who were all women representing their various fields of expertise. I was quaking by that time and was pleased I had finished drinking my coffee because I'm not sure I would have been able to get the cup to my mouth.

The meeting started with the psychiatrist confirming the information she had received from Joy and from the Sunshine Centre. We found ourselves defending Jonathan from time to time, but agreeing with the information written in the reports. My view was somewhat distorted because I felt the entire problem was caused by the fact that the school did not close its gates. Isn't love enduring? Each person was given the chance to ask us about our home situation. Questions and answers went on for a few hours, with Jonathan making a fleeting appearance to give either Barry or me a kiss, then dashing off with someone tailing him, before we'd even had time to wipe the wet kiss from our lips.

I sensed from the way the questions were posed and the responses we received, that change would result from that meeting. Questions were asked like 'How much longer do you think the family is going to be able to function normally?' and 'What effect do you think this is having on

Graeme?' and 'Do you see this as a temporary setback that is going to disappear?' Neither Barry nor I are fools. Despite the fact that our love for Jonathan clouded our acknowledgement of many realities, we knew that our family was in trouble and that change was desperately needed.

The part I always dreaded most in the assessments of Jonathan in the first seven years of his life was the summing up. It normally came with painful truths and realities and highlighted some things that needed to be changed. The summing up at that meeting at Tara and the result of it was the source of the most devastating heartache we would ever endure. In everything I have written about in this book, this part was the most upsetting for me and writing about it brought all these painful emotions to the surface. The heartache of that time will remain with me forever. The psychiatrist said, seemingly speaking on everyone's behalf, that they had seen cases like Jonathan's before and their advice was uniform in these instances. It was her belief that we had lost sight of the fact that we had lives to live and our lives were confined to ensuring Jonathan's safety. Her words rang in my ears as she said, 'You're not even being given the chance to develop this child in your efforts to keep him safe. It is our belief that your family is on the way to becoming dysfunctional and there is only one solution and that is to place Jonathan in care.' Barry and I had been expecting this, but her words still rocked us to the core. Barry reacted strongly and said quite aggressively, 'I'm not putting my child away or institutionalising him, so you can forget it.' The irony of the situation was not lost on me. The psychiatrist, who was equally arrogant and very sure of her stance, said, 'That is not what we are suggesting; we are suggesting you send your child to boarding school. Millions of children the world over go to boarding schools and spend school holidays at home!' Between the Sunshine Centre, Casa Do Sol and Tara, they had recommended making application to a school six hundred kilometres away, which was like imposing a heavy sentence on us.

In the time between being placed back at the Sunshine Centre and the assessment by Tara, I had phoned two local day schools to find out what their security measures were like and if they would accept Jonathan. Both would have required a lot of travelling but I was desperately looking for alternatives. I never found out about their security measures because both had long waiting lists for new children. The reason the school so far away was being suggested as somewhere to place him was because there were no boarding facilities locally.

With pain, anguish and much soul-searching, Barry and I sat down a few times to discuss the issue. It had to be done in stages because it was too upsetting to deal with all at the same time. Each session was cut short by one of us taking offence at one thing or another. What came out of our honest discussions was that we both felt resentful. Barry felt that he worked a long week and I expected him to look out for Jonathan over the weekends. He saw it as unfair that he could not enjoy the sport on television on a Saturday afternoon, because he had to be ripping Jonathan away from some dangerous feat. I felt that I was never off duty, even when Barry was supposedly on duty. There was never a time that I could relax, knowing Jonathan was safe, other than the hours he spent at school. I knew that if a rugby try was scored on TV, it would have Barry's full attention, and I would often have to come to Jonathan's rescue. Barry also had the tendency to fall asleep while he read the newspaper, which resulted in Jonathan running amok without any supervision. It wasn't anybody's fault; we were trying to live the life of any married couple, but with a storm raging around them. Our need to keep Jonathan safe was a symptom of the deep love we had for him. It was around this time that Jonathan fell off the swing in the garden without hurting himself, but Graeme became hysterical with fright and worry. The protectiveness Graeme feels for Jonathan comes through strongly in times of Jonathan's discomfort. Graeme would sooner have his toenails ripped out one by one than hear his brother cry.

Not enough can be said to emphasise the relationship Graeme and Jonathan have always shared. It was at about that time that Graeme accidentally put the foot of his chair on Jonathan's toe. Jonathan didn't cry and scream, as shouting was reserved for happy occasions, but he whimpered. Graeme, knowing Jonathan so well, did his usual check, almost from a mental checklist, from head to toe, to see what was causing Jonathan's expression of discomfort. He felt mortified when he realised he was responsible and had to be consoled and comforted a lot more than Jonathan did. Jonathan's injury was to the toe, Graeme's was to the soul and it took a lot longer to heal. He was full of self-loathing for causing his brother pain.

Barry and I did not discuss sending Jonathan to boarding school with Graeme, as we knew it would upset him. Until arrangements had been made and we found it within us to do it, there seemed little point in putting Graeme through unnecessary pain.

I filled in the application forms and sent them off to a school called Sunfield. As I dropped the envelope into the postbox it felt as if I was letting go of a letter arranging my own execution. It was an extremely painful decision that upended me. Along with the trauma that goes with parting with a child, particularly a child who did not talk or was not capable of taking care of himself, I felt the most overpowering sense of guilt. Nobody could possibly say the right thing. If they said they thought it was good that he was going, I'd think they didn't care about Jonathan, and if they said they thought it was bad, I'd think they didn't care about me. There was no comfort anywhere.

How we found the courage to take Jonathan by the hand and lead him up to the door of Sunfield is still beyond me. I had bought his school uniform and clothing in accordance with a list that had been posted to us. I labelled his clothing with his nametags through a veil of tears and sobs. I held him in my arms at every opportunity to apologise for what was about to happen to him. I hated myself and was angry with everyone who had suggested boarding school. How would they like to be in our shoes? We told Graeme that Jonathan was going to boarding school, but would be coming home for holidays. His response was 'But who will give him his Marmite bread?' I had to say calmly that there would be many people there to attend to all of Jonathan's needs and then removed myself to cry privately.

We were shown around the premises of Sunfield and intro-duced to the staff. The rows of beds in the large room he was to share looked clinical compared to what he was used to. We were shown where he would sleep and had the weekend to torment ourselves about taking him back on Sunday.

Just before the turn-off to the school on the highway, is a viaduct bridge. It is quite a beautiful structure, which under different circumstances would have been lovely, but whenever I saw it my heart rate changed, my hands became clammy and I became a gibbering wreck, knowing we were almost there. It amazes me how powerful negative associations can be. There is a viaduct bridge, equally lovely, just a little way from where we live and it still elicits the same reaction in me. I think it is the association of what I felt when I was on the way to dropping Jonathan at school. It never got any better.

It was by happy coincidence that we owned a small holiday flat close to Jonathan's new school, which made it possible for us, and particularly me, to spend far more time at the coast with Jonathan than we would otherwise have been able to. We had bought the flat when Jonathan was a small baby, so it was entirely familiar to him and he loved being there. The flat was a lifesaver, for a number of reasons, as it also offered security and a familiar domestic environment while we all weathered this traumatic transition.

Barry had taken a week's leave and Graeme was also with us. The plan was to leave me at the coast so that I could have Jonathan with me every weekend for the first six weeks. Jonathan seemed somehow to sense that we would be leaving him behind, as he refused to get out of the car when we got there. I was devastated by his obvious fear – he was deathly pale, whimpering pathetically, and riveted to the spot. We finally managed to get him out of the car, while Graeme jollied him along, telling him about the new friends he would make. The walk from the car to the front door seemed to go on forever. The front door of the big old house that was the hostel was locked because it was a Sunday, and as we stood waiting for someone to open it, I questioned how and why we found ourselves there. The staff on duty were clearly used to new parents and ushered us straight through to Jonathan's room and got us to unpack his clothes into his cupboard. They knew that it was best for us to leave right away, so they ushered us out smartly. Jonathan had no understanding of what was happening but he seemed to sense that this separation would be different from any others. It felt as if our hearts were being ripped out of our chests, and our emotions were strung as tight as piano wire. That moment has left a deep scar burnt forever into my heart. Perhaps it was the bewilderment in Jonathan's eyes or the sight of Barry sitting sobbing on a low wall in the school garden that made that scar so deep. The expressions on both Graeme's and Jonathan's faces made me feel like the worst kind of traitor – it was the lowest point in my life thus far.

The school insisted that we make no contact with Jonathan during the first week. We stayed at the flat that week and it was the hardest thing not being able to get a glimpse of how he was doing. We phoned and were told that he was fine and settling in well. We were invited to the school to meet Jonathan's teacher that Friday. We arrived at twelve thirty as suggested, and were directed to the small school building where his classroom was situated. At that point we were so desperate to see Jonathan that looking around the school or meeting the teacher seemed of secondary importance. Barry and I were alone, as we had sent Graeme on an outing with a friend. As we caught sight of Jonathan and he of us, he ran towards us crying and laughing at the same time. It was so wonderful to see him and Barry and I scooped him up and hugged and kissed him, oblivious to everything around us. I wonder if he had thought that he would never see us again?

The lows in life give meaning to the highs. Without all these tests, how would we know how we feel? It's been ten years since a small part of me died during those Sunfield days. How clear it is now that life has turned around for us and that small part that died within me has been filled with new hope and joy.

Chapter 20

The day we fetched Jonathan from Sunfield for the first time, we also met his new teacher, Sandy. She was a strong woman with a will that matched Jonathan's and if she said 'no' there was no confusion about it. She described her first day with Jonathan in the classroom and as she did so, it conjured up thoughts in my mind of breaking in a wild stallion. It may have been the way he vented his displeasure in being there, but he behaved, by all accounts, as if he had never been taught anything. Sandy told me that he had gone around the classroom, ripping the artwork and posters off the walls and tipping over the furniture. I think Sandy saw this as a challenge and she said she almost looked forward to his doing it again, so that she could shout 'No, Jonathan' while holding his face firmly in her hands for him to see how angry her face was.

I know Sandy would gladly have sacrificed anything Jonathan broke or spoilt, totting it up to making a break-through with him. Some months later, she was absolutely thrilled to tell me that Jonathan had climbed out of the classroom window! I looked at her while she told me this, searching her face for clues as to how I should respond. She broke into a big smile and said, 'Do you know what that means? He copied the other children doing it – he's been paying attention. He was agile enough to plan and execute it and he knew that the next step, once he was out, was to come back in through the door.' I think in reality the excitement was probably more connected to the fact that he hadn't made a dash for it when he had broken free. This was a definite breakthrough. I don't believe there could have been a better teacher for Jonathan. Her strict, no-nonsense approach was tempered by her underlying kindness. Sandy's efforts with Jonathan began on the first day and she never once gave up on him. It was her strength and perseverance that turned his serious eating problems around. I know that if what was required to get on top of that problem was to remove and withhold his food, I could never have done it. Sandy had a firm exterior that appeared to be unbending, but I know she used to bring food from home to give Jonathan as a special treat at non-meal times, being careful to keep the rules of mealtimes totally separate. She cared deeply for him and I felt secure in the knowledge that she was looking out for his welfare. It was such a relief to know that someone as empathetic and dedicated as Sandy was watching over our beloved son in our absence. We could now comfort Graeme with the knowledge that there was someone who would give Jonathan his Marmite sandwich.

Because I was staying at our flat for the first six weeks, Jonathan was able to come home with me every weekend, which was a blessing. For obvious reasons, he associated the flat with holidays and good times, so for at least two days we were able to make a pretence of having fun and good times. I found myself growing more and more morose towards lunchtime on Sundays, knowing that he needed to be back in the hostel by four o'clock. The drive to the school always made me feel physically ill, while Jonathan would sit in the back of the car, ashen, his hand in his mouth with no expression at all on his sombre little face. It occurred to me to just keep driving, irrespective of where the road would take us, and not turn off at the viaduct bridge.

For parents with children in boarding schools, the picture I am painting does seem dramatic. Sunfield was a wonderful place, the children were happy and the staff were dedicated. For many children it was the only home they knew and for others it was not their only home, but the better alternative of the two. Many of the children living in the hostel were from far away. Their families had opted for this choice because although weekly boarding would have been the ideal situation, they had no such facility near them. The personalities of some of the children seemed well adapted to group living. They loved being together and created bonds and ties that were as strong or stronger than those with their own families.

Previously, I had viewed a place like Sunfield as a home for 'don't-wants.' How wrong I was. Here was a little community that learnt to love living together, with all aspects of community living taken care of. The little church, the community hall, the vegetable gardens, the playground and the living quarters. One day I arrived to fetch Jonathan while there was a birthday party in progress. I stood at the dining room door, looking in on sixty children celebrating a little girl's birthday. I wish one of my own birthdays had felt that special! To see the faces of the children as they clapped ten times, to represent her tenth birthday, really touched me. Where else would those sixty children have learnt to be so pleased about other people's joy and good fortune? Although we were never able to come to terms with having Jonathan in a boarding school, I never lost sight of the fact that most of the children there were extremely happy.

Three weeks before my six weeks at the flat were up, Barry and Graeme made the six-hour journey to the coast as they didn't want to go through another weekend without seeing Jonathan. As I have said, the lows create the highs, and to see my boys reunited on that Friday afternoon catapulted me into a brand new high. Jonathan's face, when he got into the car, was almost luminous with joy. He, Graeme and Barry hugged and kissed, and on one level I was so happy to see their joy, but on another I felt the agony of knowing that we would inevitably be leaving him behind again.

I realise now that I was functioning under the most severe emotional strain at that time, and was unable to draw comfort or companionship from the people who cared the most about me. If people were sympathetic, I became defensive and withdrawn, and if I encountered support for my decision, I felt that they were being disloyal to Jonathan and didn't really care about his welfare. I felt terribly lonely and isolated and rejected all overtures. I was creating a protective shell to insulate myself from further hurt, and in so doing, cutting myself off from the closest people in my life, while feeling resentful that I was so alone. It was a cold and desolate place to find oneself.

I went home after six weeks, feeling a little older and a lot worse for wear. Despite the guilt Barry and I both felt, we now both admit to secretly enjoying the peace and quiet at home. I think that admission could only be made in the security of the present. Those quiet times came with a price tag, and guilt comes at an enormous cost.

Graeme's results at school in the first term of that year deteriorated sharply. We were shocked to find the comments on his school report, as they were not what we had been used to. Graeme was pale, thin and showing signs of strain. Only recently did I begin to understand how he really felt about Jonathan going to boarding school, which now explains his school performance at the time.

When I decided to write this book, I sat down with Graeme and asked him for his honest replies to my probing questions. I asked, 'Was there ever a time that you thought Jonathan was getting more attention than you or you felt left out?'

His reply, an unhesitating: 'Never!'

'Was there ever a time that you felt we did more for Jonathan than we did for you?'

'Never!'

'Was there ever a time that you resented the sort of life we were living?'

'Never!'

'Do you think there was anything we could have done differently?'

I was shattered when he looked at me, then dropped his eyes to the floor. When he raised them again, they were brimming with tears 'Why boarding school, Mom? How

161

could you have done it?' I drifted off to my bedroom and as I sat down, the tears and pain came flooding back as if it were yesterday. The terrible irony of it was that a large part of our decision to send Jonathan to boarding school was to allow us to give Graeme our undivided attention in a more tranquil atmosphere. While our objective was to protect and nurture Graeme, we were the unwitting architects of enormous stress and pain for this sensitive little boy. We did not know at that stage that the bond between the two boys went far, far deeper than that of average siblings. This close- ness is seen more often between identical twins, and the truth was that Graeme was pining. While intending to make Graeme's life easier, we had actually made it harder for him.

The first few months dragged by, with trips to the coast every three weeks to spend time together as a family. It seemed that three weeks was our tolerance limit for separation. We either went down as a family or I drove down alone. When it became difficult for all of us to go, I would go down to take Jonathan out for the weekend and could then reassure Barry and Graeme that he was fine. Luckily, cellphones came into being around that time and they could talk to Jonathan a few times during the weekend.

During the early stages of Jonathan being at Sunfield, I suffered recurrent, vivid nightmares about him drowning in a river. I think it represented the river that the viaduct bridge crossed. His ability to slip away had proven successful before, was it unthinkable that he could get out of the gates and find his way to the river? In the middle of the night it didn't feel unthinkable.

There was a strange combination in our home of gloom and

peace. I would have thought it would have been an environment in which to mend some wounds and find some inner peace. Instead, we blamed each other for meaningless days and sleepless nights. Barry blamed me for not coping and I blamed him for not helping, and without our knowledge, Graeme blamed us both for not caring. Barry and I bickered a lot. I know that we would not have survived as a family unit if it were not for our common deep love of Jonathan holding us together. In yet another example of searing irony, we had been told at Tara that we would inevitably become dysfunctional as a family if Jonathan remained at home; it was, in fact, his departure that made us dysfunctional. It was only when Jonathan came home permanently that Graeme once again became the boy we used to know.

The first six months at Sunfield were the hardest, although it got easier as Jonathan accepted and understood the routine. He knew by then that we would always come back for him. Barry and I wrote to him every week and he kept our postcards in a plastic shopping bag which he carried over his arm at all times. I felt a deep, stabbing pain when someone told me that Jonathan had cried and become aggressive when someone took his bag of cards while he was in the bath. My sisters all wrote to him regularly as well. In those six months we had been through some painful separations, with difficult scenes getting out of the car and walking through the front doorway of the hostel. We could not talk to Jonathan on the phone because he could not separate the concept of hearing our voices and yet not seeing us. If we did speak to him, he would start packing his clothes in a suitcase and would wait for us to fetch him, a picture that haunted me so much that we stopped calling him, but phoned the staff to enquire about him. Kindly, Sandy never minded if I phoned her at home for news of him.

We all longed for school holidays and always celebrated Jonathan's arrival back home, and gave him a good night out, doing the things he liked most. The same applied to the night before returning to school. These were bizarre occasions, as we were all pretending to have fun, while we knew that we were getting closer and closer to having to say goodbye. The sadness was sometimes almost unbearable.

Other parents didn't seem to be unduly affected by having their children at boarding school, and I have given a lot of thought as to why we were. I think it was because Jonathan had very limited verbal skills and had not yet developed the understanding he has today, and that made him vulnerable. He could be an infuriating child who could drive us insane with rage but we could control the rage because of our love for him. Could a caregiver do that? I also think that because we had seen him so vulnerable and fragile, hanging onto life by a thread in his times of illness, we had developed protectiveness like an umbilical cord. It was our lifeline too. The distance was a formidable barrier for us. We would have coped with weekly boarding locally if there had been such a facility, allowing us all to get on with our lives during the week and maintain contact over the weekends.

The coast became an integral part of my life. When I was away, I longed to be there because when I was there I had Jonathan. That positive association lives with me and still holds some comfort for me, even though Jonathan has lived inland with us for years now. We lived from one visit to the next and I existed just to plan my next trip.

There is nothing much more to tell about the two years Jonathan spent at Sunfield. I had been phoning Joy, the headmistress of Casa Do Sol, periodically in the hope that Jonathan's name had made some progress up the waiting list. I had assured her that we were dealing with a different Jonathan. I knew the waiting list was the reason, but Joy's memory of running after Jonathan down a busy road while he was turning back scoffing and jeering at her, could not have strengthened his case.

Jonathan had made a lot of progress at Sunfield. He was eating much better and not dashing away as he used to. We had started to be kinder to ourselves, finding comfort in the fact that this needed to happen to make him more manageable. We will never know what part of that change was due to extremely firm rules and what part to maturity.

I have a vivid picture in my mind of Barry getting onto his knees to say goodbye to Jonathan. This put him at eye level and hugging proximity. When you're six foot four inches tall, a seven-year-old child is small in comparison. That picture has always reminded me of a quote from the Knights of Pythagoras: 'A man never stands as tall as when he kneels to help a child.'

Chapter 21

It came as a shock when Sandy told us she was leaving Sunfield to teach at another school. I immediately found that I had another reason to lie awake at night, worrying how we would manage without Sandy.

I asked about her new post and she told me very enthusiastically about the challenges of her new job. She took me to see the school, Golden Hours, which wasn't very far from Sunfield. Because it had originally been built as a school, the entire facility had an ordered appearance. I was mildly interested in it for Sandy's sake but it did not cross my mind that Jonathan could follow Sandy there. Once the possibility had occurred to us, we set the wheels in motion, and the result was that Jonathan was accepted at Golden Hours and put in Sandy's class. Prior to making the decision to move him from Sunfield to Golden Hours, I had once again approached Joy about the waiting list for Casa Do Sol, with negative results.

The move to Golden Hours was easier than I expected. I don't think I ever got over the day we first took Jonathan to Sunfield through that painful viaduct archway. I didn't hate the place, but I hated the feeling it gave me. The adjustment to Jonathan's living away from home had been made. Another two years went on like this.

Golden Hours was good for Jonathan. Sandy took a personal interest in him and helped him develop in a number of ways. This was when we discovered that Jonathan needed to wear glasses. Happily, his stay at Golden Hours was relatively uneventful, except for two incidents, both of which involved his glasses. On the first occasion, Jonathan had climbed onto the school roof and, in an attempt to get himself out of trouble, claimed that he went up there to find his glasses. He had no explanation as to why the glasses were up there in the first place. On another occasion his glasses went missing and were found some time later buried in the garden. Hercule Poirot himself would never have been able to unravel this mystery.

Soon after Jonathan started at Golden Hours, the subject of tranquillising medication was brought up. I can't remember who recommended it or why, but I seem to think that the staff were having trouble controlling him in the hostel. I decided to bring him home for assessment in order to monitor the effects of his medication, Melleril. I noticed little change, but the hostel reported an improvement in his behaviour. After approximately a year, I decided to stop the medication, as I noticed he had developed a tremor. He still has that tremor today, so it clearly had nothing to do with the drug. When we had stopped giving him the medication I could detect no discernible difference.

Not long after his stay at home to get settled on Melleril, Jonathan started having trouble with one of his knees. His kneecap would slip out of place to one side, a symptom of his low muscle tone. It had been happening for a long time, but he had started falling when the kneecap slipped out of place and could no longer hold him up. He needed surgery to have it fixed and has had no trouble with it since. He settled back at school after six weeks at home in a cast. I thought having him in plaster of Paris was going to be a nightmare, but he shuffled along the floor on his bottom as if he had never done anything else. Jonathan has always accepted his fate without question. When the plaster cast was removed six weeks later, I was shocked to see the size of the wound and it amazed me that he had handled it so well. What I remember most about the knee operation was him falling into a friend's swimming pool one night when we were visiting, and trying to get the cast dry with a hairdryer.

On the surface, we had settled into a tolerable routine, and there wasn't a particular incident that made me get up one morning and say, 'I'm fetching Jonathan today. I have had enough!' The cheers of delight from Barry and Graeme made me wish that I had been able to make the decision earlier. We had travelled a long and painful road and the day had finally arrived when we could no longer bear life without Jonathan. Within two hours I had started the six hundred kilometre journey to fetch him. I had no idea what we would do about a school and, frankly, I couldn't have cared less. If we had to consider home or private tutoring, well, so be it. I phoned the principal of Golden Hours and told her I was on my way and all his possessions were to be ready when I got there. We stayed overnight at the flat and drove back the following day with liberated souls; the chains had been removed. We were unshackled! Throughout the journey home, I found myself bursting into song and laughter for no reason. Jonathan kept clapping his hands, and the atmosphere was electric.

We arrived home later that afternoon to Barry and Graeme, who had been anxiously and excitedly awaiting our arrival; Barry had come home early from work to celebrate the occasion. Graeme and Jonathan danced around the kitchen, laughing and singing hysterically, while Barry and I embraced, sharing feelings of deep relief and happiness that our family was once again a unit. We hadn't had time to make any plans and we had no idea what the future would hold, but we knew without the slightest doubt that we had done the right thing. Jonathan belonged at home, with us.

Euphoria reigned in our house for a few weeks. I phoned Joy to check the status of the now-even-more-important waiting list, to be told that there was no change. The only school I had not yet approached, because of its rather remote location, was Gateway. If he was not accepted there, I would need to consider home schooling, a system I am not very keen on. Knowing how much Jonathan has learnt from other children confirmed my view that isolating him from a school environment would grossly hamper his development. I think the headmistress of Gateway saw the desperation in my eyes, and Jonathan started there on the first day of the next term. When I dropped him off for his first day, his pale, defeated expression made me realise that he probably thought he was being abandoned in a strange place once again. How wonderful it was for all of us when he realised that he would come home again every single day.

Gateway was about fifteen kilometres from our home and Graeme's school was equally far in the opposite direction. It took me three hours each day to drop and fetch them both but this was a small price to pay for the calm that came over our family. I joined a lift club, which helped a great deal, and we slipped back into the mundane and boring routine that we had so yearned for. Although our household could never be called peaceful or normal, we were all happy.

Things had not changed in that Jonathan was still hyperactive and, of course, still had Down syndrome. He came home from boarding school improved in many ways, but on occasion he could be as stubborn and unmanageable as ever. If he decided that he was going to sit flat on the floor in the middle of the supermarket aisle and do the dance of joy, there was very little to be done about it. He was too big to pick up and too stubborn to hear any pleas. Cathy started having Jonathan over for weekends which gave us a break from time to time. I think she could see that Barry and I had very little time to ourselves and needed some time out. Not many people would have taken on the challenge and we were always grateful and aware that her relationship with Jonathan was a special one.

Our household dynamics were far from what is found in most other homes, but because of that, so many other things were also different. We never had bickering and squabbling. We didn't have a problem with 'keep out of my room' or 'he's got more than I have' or 'you care less about me'. Most households have some aspect of that at some point; we never did. Graeme always backed us in our praise or discipline and never showed any signs of feeling left out.

The highlight of Jonathan's time at Gateway was a truly magnificently staged concert. He played the part of an elephant and had the most beautiful costume that someone had put time and trouble into making. That concert stands out in my mind not purely for the memories I have of Jonathan coming onto the stage and walking around, lost because he couldn't see past his trunk, but because of a scene performed by a younger class. There was a group of very small girls, about three years old, with Down syndrome, dressed in white tutus with halos and wings that looked as though they had been born with them. They looked so much like little angels that it seemed as though the halos didn't need the piece of wire to hold them up. That is the picture I have of heaven – pure white innocence. However, knowing how spontaneous and uninhibited young children with Down syndrome can be, there was always the nerve-racking possibility of unscripted dialogue that could be particularly shocking coming from the lips of cherubs. The videotape of that concert remains a huge favourite in our house, and Jonathan can still recite word for word and note for note every moment of that concert.

I am eternally grateful that I was able to see this wonderful concert – the little girls in white epitomised for me the spirit of Down syndrome – purity, innocence and beauty. I realised that, but for Jonathan, I may not have had the opportunity to have those pictures stored in my mind.

Chapter 22

Barry travelled to England from time to time because his company's head office was situated just outside London. A trip had been scheduled for a conference that he was to attend, and we decided that I would join him for a week to see London again and meet up with the people who had become a second family to me twenty years before. Barry would leave first and I would join him after his conference. I would spend a week with him and he would return, while I would stay on with my surrogate family for another week.

We were becoming more and more excited about our trip, as we planned to go to the theatre, dine out, and see the sights of London. These plans meant that the boys would be without either of their parents at home for one week only. Tickets were booked and reservations made, right down to theatre tickets. Barry left as planned and as the week progressed, I started to feel a little uncomfortable about us both being away at the same time. We had become used to doing things in shifts so that at least one of us was holding the fort. Jonathan was not the sort of child that you could take to someone's door and say, 'Oh, just keep him for me for a couple of days.' Trips like this had to be finely orchestrated – lifts, meals, emergency backups, and more. Helen and

Graeme could take care of everything with help from the family.

Two days before I was due to depart, Jonathan complained of a sore stomach and a headache. I presumed it was a headache because he said his hair was sore. Jonathan has an exceptionally high pain threshold and together with his lack of verbal skills, it was difficult to know when there was a problem.

The day before I was due to leave, he had a high fever and was lethargic. I wondered if it would be wise to leave him, and when Barry phoned later that night, I asked him whether I should cancel the ticket right away in order to get some sort of refund. We agreed that we would wait until the morning. Jonathan seemed much better the following morning, but I decided to keep him out of school and to take him to see our doctor. I was unable to contact one of the lift club members, so I had no choice but to take the other children to school and take Jonathan to the doctor afterwards. On the way back from the school I could see Jonathan's condition was rapidly deteriorating, and sped to the doctor's rooms as fast as morning traffic would allow.

I managed to carry him into the doctor's rooms and he lay on the floor in the waiting room, unable to move, his legs pulled tightly up to his chest. The doctor examined him where he lay and immediately sent us to the hospital to see a surgeon she had contacted in the interim. Jonathan was a large twelve-year-old by this time and I had to carry him to and from the car each time. How strength comes to you when you need it most! He was seen by the surgeon and was prepared for surgery straight away as the surgeon could not make a diagnosis without operating. He indicated the need for a drip to be put up immediately. I froze. 'A drip?' 'Yes,' he said. 'We'll have to start medicating him straight away.' In a pathetic voice I said, 'He won't let you.' He replied, 'Well, what do you suggest? We have to put up a drip.' I looked at him and repeated, 'He won't let you.' He dismissed my comment and rushed back to the operating theatre he'd just left, obviously irritated.

Jonathan was taken to a ward, where he fought like a tiger every time anyone came near him. He desperately wanted something to drink. He had brought up any liquid he had in his system and was obviously dehydrating, which is probably why he needed a drip. He would not give a urine specimen and they could not get a temperature reading from him. A sister from the laboratory came to draw blood and they soon found out what I had tried to warn them of. He wouldn't let them. The surgeon was called and came flying into the ward, saying to the accompanying ward sister, 'We'll have to get the drip up in theatre.' As he was leaving, Jonathan said 'juice' and the surgeon called over his shoulder, 'Don't give this child anything to drink.' While Jonathan was being X-rayed, I phoned Cath to ask her to arrange for someone else to do the school lifts and then phoned Barry in London. There was silence on the other end of the phone for a few seconds, until he'd gathered himself enough to say, 'I'm coming home.'

Cathy stayed with me while Jonathan was in theatre. It felt like a few days rather than a few hours. He was wheeled back semi-conscious and fighting like a demon. He was too strong to be tied down and had pulled the oxygen tube out of his nose and if his hands hadn't been bandaged into mitts, he'd have pulled his drip out as well. Jonathan was angry, frightened and obviously in pain. He thrashed around, making it very hard for me to keep the oxygen mask near his face. The sister came in several times to ask: 'Has he passed urine yet?' which he hadn't. The surgeon eventually arrived to check on him and explained to me what he'd found. Jonathan's appendix had ruptured a few days earlier and he had septicaemia and peritonitis. Later that day the surgeon returned and he said that nursing Jonathan had become too difficult and they would have to put him into an induced coma in order to be able to treat him. Stunned, exhausted and distraught, I walked alongside Jonathan while he was wheeled into the intensive care unit. When we got to the door, a squat woman with a thoroughly unpleasant scowl snorted, 'You can't come in here. I suggest you go away for about an hour while we work with your child.'

I decided to go home, as the hospital was only a few blocks away, planning to return within half an hour. When I got home I phoned Barry, who was so choked up that he couldn't talk and had to phone me back, by which time he told me that he was booked on that evening's flight. While I was on the phone to Barry, the surgeon had been trying to locate me. He expressed extreme irritation that I had not been given a Procedures Consent form to sign, without which he refused to proceed. I rushed back to the hospital and waited outside the intensive care unit for what felt like an eternity. The surgeon finally emerged, saying, 'Okay, he's fine. Come in and I'll explain what we've done.' I found myself standing next to Jonathan, who was attached to a respirator that was breathing for him, he had various medications attached to his drip, drains out of his wound, an oxygen tube up his nose, a catheter inserted and was drugged into unconsciousness. I looked at him in absolute horror. The surgeon looked confused and said, 'Why are you crying?' Did he think I was going to be pleased? I had lost my arm in this hospital, Jonathan had been born there, and he had also been seriously ill with pneumonia there a number of times. Those hospital walls had been an emotional prison for me many times.

I stood next to Jonathan's bed for a while. I was not made to feel very welcome in the unit, as I think it was fairly unusual to have children there.

There seemed little point in sitting watching Jonathan sleep while Graeme was at home, so after visiting time in the hospital I went home. Barry arrived the next morning and drove straight from the airport to the hospital, where I met him. I could see the strain on his face. He was horrified to see Jonathan – it is a shock for any parent to see their child in that state, but for us his immobility was haunting. We were not used to holding Jonathan's hand and talking to him calmly, the way we could as he lay there in a coma. If he had been awake, he would surely have pulled his hand away and dashed off.

He was being treated with a powerful dose of antibiotics to get the infection under control and because he was comatose, there was no evidence of any improvement. Graeme's distress throughout the entire ordeal had been heartbreaking in itself. I remember fetching him from school while Jonathan was under anaesthetic the day he got sick. Graeme's face first showed disbelief, then deep distress. I found it hard to console him and tell him everything would be all right, because I wasn't sure that it would be. It always struck me at those times how different our household was from most.

While all my friends with children of the same age were complaining of incessant fighting and bickering between siblings, we were blessed with Graeme and Jonathan's devotion to each other.

Days went by, with Jonathan still in an induced coma. The surgeon assured us that Jonathan's treatment was going according to plan, but he was evasive and considered the details regarding Jonathan's condition to be none of our business. It must be apparent that I have had a few run-ins with certain doctors, but this is not because I am overprotective and pushy. It was always because doctors appeared to view the treatment of children with Down syndrome as less important.

I have so often come up against a subliminal or unconscious attitude from ignorant people. For some inexplicable reason, they seem to believe that the degree of love that parents feel is in direct proportion to the degree of disability. The greater the perceived imperfection, the less lovable the child must be. In fact, the exact opposite applies. The parent has to assume a great number of functions that the child cannot perform alone, and is therefore connected to the child almost as a lifeline. Losing the child would be like losing a huge part of oneself. You talk for him, you think for him, and you dream for him, resulting in a bond that is indestructible and totally unique.

After six days it was decided that they would try to get Jonathan breathing on his own again, so they attempted to remove the ventilator. It was not successful, as he could not breath unaided and the doctor had to be called, amid enormous panic, to reinsert the pipe down his throat and medicate him into a deep sleep again. He seemed to get worse from then on, and by the next day the surgeon was saying that Jonathan's kidneys were not functioning as well as they should be and as a result he was retaining fluid. He became swollen and puffy. We were in a panic as we could see that his condition was rapidly deteriorating. We were then told that he had pneumonia as well. That night there was a new staff member on duty who told us that Jonathan's catheter had been blocked yet again, explaining the kidney failure. It was intolerable to me that Jonathan's discomfort and our anguish could have been avoided by something so obvious. This was the second time a blocked catheter had gone undetected. The following morning I collared the surgeon, and we ended up exchanging extremely heated words. This is always counterproductive, and we both calmed down to have a more rational discussion. I reminded him that I had spoken for, lived for and dreamed for Jonathan for the last twelve years, and would have breathed for him in the previous eight days if I could have. For this reason, I desperately needed to know what was happening.

Perhaps he thought about what I had said, because there was a pause before he replied, 'Do you understand that you have a very sick child?'

In spite of the sometimes difficult circumstances, I have that unit to thank for Jonathan's recovery. I would choose the same doctor again, because I think he is a very good one, and I would hope that our little encounter would improve his bedside manner.

On day ten the respirator was removed, the sedating medication was stopped, and Jonathan regained consciousness. He was put into a ward and was there for another two days before effecting his miracle recovery trick. This entails a metamorphosis from being deathly ill to almost robustly healthy in no time at all. While I was feeling emotionally wrung out, Mr Congeniality was charming the nurses and ready for a party.

It was a joyous day when we took him home, as I had wondered if he would ever see the inside of our home again.

Chapter 23

Jonathan was eventually well enough to return to Gateway and things returned to a wonderful mundane normality. Within a few months, we were surprised to get a call from Joy at Casa Do Sol. The parents of a child attending the school were relocating and would find it more convenient to place their child at Gateway. The principals of both schools conspired to come up with a suggestion that was music to our ears. They proposed that a direct swap be effected, whereby the two children would simply replace each other in the same classes. As it was late in the year, it was decided that Jonathan would start at Casa Do Sol in the new year.

This was the most wonderful news we had received in years; Casa Do Sol is close to our home and was a known entity. We had started despairing that Jonathan would ever be accepted again, so this was cause for great celebration.

It felt like going home. It had been five years since Jonathan's first day at Casa Do Sol and a very different boy was returning. His days at boarding school had accustomed him to being part of a group and accepting and respecting authority. He had also learnt that if he didn't eat his food, there was a table full of children waiting to eat it for him.

When he started at Casa Do Sol, Jonathan went into Lindi's class. Lindi is a no-nonsense kind of teacher and keeps very good control in the classroom. She recognises the children's capabilities and pushes them to their fullest potential. Barry and I went to parents' evening in the first year and Lindi showed us Jonathan's books. We were flabbergasted and could scarcely believe our eyes. Jonathan had reported his weekend activities to Lindi, she had written it all out on paper, and he had traced over her writing into his own book. Can you imagine how we felt when we saw written in his book things like 'I swam with my Dad and we went out for a pizza on Saturday', when it had actually happened? It was an electrifying moment; our boy was learning to write.

Lindi had advised us that the weekly sporting activity was ice skating and that I was to dress Jonathan warmly on Thursdays. I smirked to myself at the thought of Jonathan ice skating. He was never very steady on his feet at the best of times and has always stubbornly resisted new experiences. I was reasonably certain he would thoroughly enjoy the bus ride to the ice rink, and that would be his only voluntary participation. How wrong I was. Before long he was on the rink with skates on, clinging to the railing, and moving along. I was invited to accompany the group shortly after he had mastered his balance and could scarcely believe my eyes. He was skating, albeit precariously, right across the rink, on his own. He adamantly refused assistance and his expression was one of determination. Every time Lindi tried to take his hand, he yanked it away, insisting 'Myself!' My heart burst with pride.

Feeling proud of our children was becoming something of a habit. A few years before, Graeme had been nominated as head boy of his school, and had excelled at swimming. However, the proudest moment ever was at a major sports event during Graeme's final school year. We were sitting on the sidelines when Graeme came looking for Jonathan. He took him by the hand and walked across the sports field with him to join his friends, oblivious of any looks or reactions that may have been directed their way. He has always spontaneously demonstrated his deep devotion to his younger brother, irrespective of where he is or who is present. This kind of sensitivity and maturity is rare for a boy of seventeen.

It seems that honesty and open discussion about a sibling with a disability paves the way for a natural relationship to develop. It stands to reason that if the parents were apprehensive about talking about it openly, the sibling would develop feelings of embarrassment and shame. While the late teens and early twenties are characterised by self-absorption and being engrossed by appearances and how others perceive them, there is a test that siblings of disabled children often pass. They are able to set aside all the rules they apply to themselves and their friends and out of compassion can adjust those rules to suit their sibling's circumstances. It is no wonder they emerge as better individuals with a greater capacity to care about others.

When Graeme was in his final year of junior school, his classmates thought it was a joke to pass a message down the line while they were queued up to file into the classroom. 'Graeme's brother looks like a monkey, Graeme's brother looks like a monkey' was repeated until it reached his ears. I was told this story by one of his friends. He never mentioned it, nor did he remember it when I reminded him of it. I think his relationship with his brother was strong enough then, even at such a vulnerable age, to disregard what anyone said or thought. His attitude towards his brother was impervious to what others thought. Graeme showed maturity in that he didn't run home crying, 'They called my brother a monkey.' He rose above it; his maturity and wisdom at twelve years old made him different from his peers.

There was never a recurrence of Jonathan trying to get out of the gate after he returned to Casa Do Sol. By that time he had more sense and understood that some things were not allowed. Lindi treated all the children in her class the same way, but I noticed that she was particularly protective of Jonathan. She was defensive if he was blamed for things she believed he had been put up to. Some of the boys in his class, who were physically and verbally more advanced, would occasionally spur him on to do something dangerous or outrageous, and he would do it in a frenzied burst of activity and then get into trouble. This normally happened in the playground and I quite often found him in Joy's office, doing punishment time for bad behaviour, when I fetched him from school.

Lindi had been working on Jonathan's fine motor co-ordination by showing him how to cut out shapes with scissors. At the time I was doing some dressmaking and had cut out a pair of slacks. When I returned to work on them, I was vexed to find a large shape cut out of one of the legs. Even more annoying was that Jonathan had cut out an almost perfect circle, something he had not previously come close to. However, there was no reward for fine motor ability in this instance.

Jonathan spent two years in Lindi's class before moving on to an older class. Children at Casa Do Sol are grouped together in classrooms according to their ages, not their ability. The teacher has to work with individuals at their own pace, keeping track of what each child is capable of. It is not an easy task and I admire the people who choose this career.

The next year Jonathan moved on to Jeanet's class. The weekly sporting activity in her class was horse riding. Jonathan has always had an unreasonable and phobic fear of animals. He would literally wet his pants if a dog sidled up to him. I have never understood his fear, but recognise it as a phobia based on the absolute terror he registers if he is near animals. It is the same travelling down escalators, although going up is fine. To get him on a 'down' escalator you would have to move heaven and earth. He developed this fear fairly recently for no apparent reason. When Jeanet said they were going horse riding I had a stronger feeling about it than when Lindi told me they were going ice skating. I envisaged horse riding as being threatening to Jonathan and something he would even hate watching. I was sent a form to be filled in by the parents of riders, an indemnity in case of injury. I didn't even bother to fill it in because I knew Jonathan would not participate. I was wrong again! He was involved at first with grooming the horses, and loved it so much that Jeanet insisted that I get an X-ray of his neck to confirm that it was safe for him to ride, which was a prerequisite on the part of the riding school. Jonathan climbed onto a horse and was walked around on it. Horse riding day was the highlight of his week for that entire year.

He could not ride on his own, but it was a breakthrough that he would permit close contact with an animal, particularly one so big. It has taught me to never say never.

We probably all look at our children ten years down the line and marvel at what they have become. Human development is a miracle. Perhaps for us, whose children do not develop in a uniform and expected way, the miracle feels even greater. It may be thought that the opposite is true, that talk of miracles is inappropriate to late development and delayed speech. But this is wrong; waiting makes one patient and tolerant and appreciative. Waiting stops you from taking anything for granted. When little legs are malformed and hands are misshapen, the miracles of walk and play seem magnified. When small mouths are deformed and brain pathways are damaged, the sound of speech is glorious. These children make us stop and assess the purpose of life. In the wise words of the Dalai Lama, 'Whether we are rich or poor, educated or uneducated, whatever our nationality, colour, social status or ideology may be, the purpose of our lives is to be happy.' I think the test at the end of our lives is not how much money we have in the bank, or how close we have come to reaching our goals, but what we have achieved in the pursuit of happiness. What advantage is there to being wealthy, but unhappy? What reason is there for being a parent if great joy does not come with the responsibility?

We look at Jonathan's face every day and are reminded of what happiness looks like. When Jonathan is involved in an event at school, the question Barry and Graeme ask is not 'Was he good at it?' but rather 'Did he love it?' The focus is not on personal perfection, but rather the purpose of life, to be happy. Jonathan has made us move our own goalposts to value happiness more fully, and put achievement into perspective. It has changed our values and increased our humility. If it wasn't for Jonathan, we may have missed it all.

I believe everybody has a talent and for those who don't think they do, I suggest that it has not yet been discovered and that they should continue to look for it. Jonathan's talent is rhythm. He is part of a drumming group at school, where they play African Djembe drums. His talent was only discovered this year by his drumming teacher Chris, who brought this gift into the lives of the children at Casa Do Sol. I love watching the children beat away at their drums with incredible skill and precision, knowing just when to beat and when to stop, all in time with each other. There is something very therapeutic about playing the drums. Perhaps it is the freedom of expression they offer, as well as permission to make that sort of noise. Freedom of expression could, however, be demonstrated more quietly at four-thirty in the morning!

The feast day of St John the Baptist is celebrated in a special way at Casa Do Sol every year. They call it the St John's Festival of light and love. Each child makes a lantern as a class activity, and the lanterns are all lit and placed on the stage in the hall when the parents arrive in the evening. Each class has a turn to stage a performance, whether it be singing, dancing or playing musical instruments. After that everyone proceeds outside, taking their lanterns with them, and sits around a bonfire singing the traditional St John's songs. My heart almost leapt out of my chest with pride as I watched Jonathan lead the drumming, play a xylophone and sing louder than anyone else that night. There could not have been a prouder parent watching, especially in view of the fact that Jonathan had previously needed to be carried in, pushed, jostled along or herded in a group to be part of a performance. Here he was now, independent, confident and very good at what he was doing.

Something occurred to me that night that I have watched out for ever since and it has been confirmed a number of times. I don't know exactly when it happened, but Jonathan seemed to have caught up with the other people of his age with Down syndrome. I know some of them read and write and Jonathan doesn't. His behaviour is often more rowdy and uncontrolled, but when I see them all in a group, Jonathan fits in perfectly. The gap that had always existed has narrowed. Perhaps I could have been spared the panic and pain of his not keeping up with his contemporaries, but if I had been spared, I would not have had this overwhelming feeling of accomplishment when seeing him interacting and laughing with his friends. He has learnt things differently, but he's learnt them nonetheless.

Chapter 24

A journey is the act of travelling from one place to another. Jonathan's journey definitely took him to a very different place. The chapters of this book describe his journey, but let me tell you now a little about the destination, although that word suggests that it's the end of the journey, which it is not. It's only the end of my story.

Jonathan is now eighteen years old. He is six feet tall and a well-built boy with typical Down syndrome characteristics. There is no mistaking him for anything else. He walks awkwardly, but with determination and usually has a destination in mind. His speech is not clear, although he generally makes himself understood. He is tolerant of the fact that not everyone understands him first time round. I know this because I have often heard him talking to his make-believe telephone call recipients and he says things like, 'I'm going to school. No – school. No – school!' He makes allowances for his speech disability even in his fantasy world. We, at home, understand everything he says and only occasionally have to consult each other to make sure we have understood him. Like a lot of people with Down syndrome, his speech sounds flat because of his raised palate and large tongue, but he also occasionally stammers and battles to get words out. He quite often stamps one foot in his attempt to spit the word out, but is never bad-tempered with frustration or the time it takes. Occasionally he finds it humorous when he's tried to say 'Mom' and he says, 'Mo . . . Mo . . . Mo' and it has not been forthcoming. He laughs and says 'Oh, sorry' and tries again. A friend was recently trying to take a photograph of him and made the mistake of asking him to say 'cheese'. In his attempt to get the word out, he was stamping his foot gently and although the 'cheese' smile was perfect, his movements were not conducive to taking a good photograph.

Jonathan wears glasses because he is shortsighted. He also has a condition called nystagmus, which causes his eyes to shiver and shake, blurring his vision slightly. This means he needs to sit very close to the television screen to be able to see the picture. He has the characteristic spots on his irises that many people with Down syndrome have. He smiles most of the time, laughs some of the time and shouts and shrieks with delight a lot of the time. With the drum, guitar, CD player, shouting and singing, our home is very noisy. Not a place you'd go if you wanted to reflect quietly on life, but definitely a place you'd go if you wanted to hear what happiness sounds like. You'd see a colourful side of human behaviour and you'd feel extremely welcome.

Jonathan is going through a developmental stage at the age of eighteen which genetically normal children go through at about four or five years old. He has imaginary friends, makes pretend phonecalls and gives long speeches, which include introducing imaginary guests with intermittent applause. Fantasy is a stage of development that gives a child practice for real life situations. They act out interactions with others that they use later on in life. Jonathan's total lack of inhibition allows him to be in his fantasy world without feeling foolish or silly. He often walks alongside me in a public place and talks on his imaginary cell phone with the finger aerial, and I don't notice until someone almost falls over themselves staring. Barry wouldn't stop him and would probably say the person staring looked a lot sillier with his mouth hanging open and his eyes out on stalks. I would argue that I don't want Jonathan to be noticed in public, but rather to blend into the environment by behaving appropriately.

Jonathan is extremely friendly and affectionate. We have had to teach him who to be affectionate with. Family and friends have always accepted his warmth and closeness, but strangers and acquaintances are often threatened by it, particularly as he has grown older. People with Down syndrome have the ability to attach themselves to the significant people in their lives and their loyalty remains steadfast. It is a myth that they are unable to form close interpersonal relationships, and they show their love in a very demonstrative way. It can be threatening for a woman to be approached by what appears to be a grown-up man who, in his innocence, flings his arms around her. Perhaps that is where one of the myths about males with Down syndrome began. Many people I have spoken to believe that they have a higher than normal sex drive. I presume that is what they are referring to when they say they are over-sexed. It's a ridiculous myth with absolutely no foundation. Often, as in Jonathan's case, they are little boys trapped in men's bodies. They are also, unlike girls with Down syndrome, infertile. Only one case has ever been recorded of a male with Down syndrome fathering a child. In the case of the girls, they have a fifty-fifty chance of having a genetically normal child, because of the fact that the child could only have a non-Down syndrome father.

I would love to know where these myths about mentally disabled people come from. It seems there are two facts people who know little about Down syndrome are sure of, they are happy and they are musical. They have feelings and talents like everyone else. They do have a tendency to be good-natured, but are equally susceptible to disappointment and can just as easily be hurt as any of us. They are not necessarily musical but often have a great love for music.

No matter how scrawny Jonathan became, his chubby, cherubic little face radiated love and happiness whatever he was doing. His slanted eyes and the flatness of the bridge of his nose are what make his appearance so different. I have never come across a person with Down syndrome who does not have beautiful, deep, warm and kind eyes. It must be these characteristics that give them their happy and con-tented appearance. People with Down syndrome have no capacity for malicious thought. This doesn't mean that they are not capable of being unpleasant or angry, but the difference between maliciousness and unpleasantness is that the first requires intent and the second is a learnt response. It is so comfortable to embrace a person who you know is good to the core. They are never going to question your judgement or motives or consider you a fool. They share your life, thinking you are wonderful and completely without fault, accepting your word and imitating your actions. This creates a kind of self-perpetuating mutual admiration society, as it is human nature to be flattered and kindly disposed towards someone who is attempting to emulate your every move.

Mentioning Down syndrome facial characteristics reminds me of an incident which happened while we were on a visit to a game park when Jonathan was not quite a year old and Graeme was four. We were having breakfast at an outside dining area and Graeme appeared to be distracted. He kept giving quick discreet glances over my shoulder at a group of people at another table. I asked him what he was looking at, and he leant forward towards Barry and me and confidentially whispered into his cupped hands, 'Don't look now, but there is a table full of people – all Down's!' I looked around, wondering if I would recognise anyone, and was paralysed with silent mirth to see a large group of Japanese people enjoying their breakfast, oblivious of Graeme's misplaced empathy.

Jonathan has always been a very sociable child, and loves visitors and visiting. The grand welcome he always gives people never leaves any doubt as to how pleased he is to see them. Whenever we visit my mom, he starts calling 'Granny, Granny' before I've even parked the car. I'm sure the neighbours think there is an emergency, with his frantic calling, but Granny knows that it is only the urgent sound of pleasure. He loves people, but has always reserved a special place for those who truly care about him. He hugs Pennie, one of his aunts, in a different way and he kisses Cathy knowing she's not going to say 'Yuk, that was a wet one.' I'm reminded of one of his earlier birthday parties, when he was due to blow out the candles. His overenthusiastic blow unfortunately contained a mouthful of saliva as well, and the candles were all extinguished, but not by his breath. Strangely, no one seemed very hungry after that.

Jonathan's love knows no distance. He loves Pat and Mike

unreservedly and the same goes for Margaret and Greg, two of my sisters and their husbands who live in other countries. Near or far, it's the true unconditional acceptance of who he is, that counts.

Jonathan loves everything familiar. I'm sure he considers characters from television sitcoms to be part of his extended family. He loves watching Walt Disney films over and over again, feeling very pleased with himself when he knows what is going to happen next and he knows all the words of the songs. He only has to watch it once to learn the words. One night he was singing our national anthem while I was preparing dinner and when he was done, he sang the entire Australian national anthem. Barry was just outside the kitchen and came back to confirm what he was hearing, while I stood there speechless. We worked out that he had learnt it from watching international rugby matches with his dad. The words were not very clear, but there was no mistaking, 'Advance, Australia Fair!' He is observant and his impish sense of humour and ability to mimic can be very enter-taining. There is a very fine line between laughing with Jonathan and laughing at him. He is not sensitive to people laughing at him, but I am. I can tell if the fun has turned into ridicule and I normally remove him from the situation by distracting him or changing the focus.

I was recently in a shop with Jonathan where the grocery packer was a young albino boy of about eighteen. Jonathan recognised that he was different and did a double take. He then moved closer to him, looking over the top of his glasses to get a clearer view, and moved forward until he was vir-tually nose to nose. I froze, not knowing what Jonathan was going to say or do. But Jonathan put his hand out to shake the boy's and said, 'I'm Jonathan, how're you doing?' It made me think how nice it would be if people who did not clearly understand what they were looking at when they looked at Jonathan, would deal with it as he had. Jonathan has often shown empathy. This is probably one of the few things that he has not been taught, but something that comes from within.

He is extremely affectionate and I recently watched him gently stroking the back of my mother's hands saying, 'Ah, Granny, nice Granny.' That is one of the nice things about Jonathan, you know that what he says he really means, because he does not have the capacity to have hidden agendas or ulterior motives. Jonathan spends time on his own quite a lot now. He has become independent and enjoys spending time in his room listening to music, playing his musical instruments, or playing with some of the figurines that have become favourites. His fantasy world makes his games come alive and he acts out situations with the popular toy figurines such as Spiderman, pretending to be each of them in turn. It always strikes me, when I hear him in his room, happily playing and entertaining himself, that he has come a vast distance. It seems like yesterday that our lives were spent solely watching him and ensuring his safety. I feel that Jonathan can enjoy life now, without me trying to improve his ability every hour of every day. He's earned the right to not spend every minute being educated. I feel that school is enough and when he comes home he should do what he enjoys and chooses to do. I am constantly paying attention to his life skills and social behaviour, but it is bliss these days to relax and watch Jonathan making progress and learning from experiences on his own.

I have the utmost respect for families who choose to do intensive high-pressure home programmes with their disabled children. They are selfless and very dedicated, and I used to wonder if it would have benefited Jonathan in any way if I had done the same. I would not have wanted to put Jonathan through the constant and ongoing pulling and pushing that is required, particularly in view of his regular bouts of ill health. Nor would I have wanted to put the family through more than we were already experiencing. Therapy and training are essential, but I think therapy can take many forms. For instance, an expedition to the supermarket can be as beneficial as many formal therapy activities. One can teach a child to make choices by asking what products he prefers. Counting can be encouraged by counting out fruit and vegetables as you put them into bags. It is a good place to point out that they can't have everything they want off the sweet counter, and taking turns can be demonstrated as you wait in the queue to pay. Many processes of daily living can simulate some of the exercises in the therapy room, but the difference is that the child is getting a more relevant understanding of life when they are out in the real world. Simultaneously, he is spending time with a parent, and is being seen and acknowledged by a society that may have had little understanding that disabled children do have value. Thus, while he is learning, he is providing lessons of his own. Taking Jonathan out to public places with me has made me realise that higher visibility will help to develop society's tolerance and understanding.

I know that Jonathan will need to be cared for for the rest of his life. He is never going to be totally independent. I had to come to this sad realisation very early on in his life, and when I was agonising over it, I imagined that he would always remain the same as he was then. What unbounded joy it was for us to watch his huge progress over the years. He has, in fact, in a number of ways, become more independent than I ever imagined he could be. He is extremely fastidious about his personal hygiene, showering or bathing at least twice a day, and he has a daily routine of carefully selecting his clothes for the day, which always match or go well together, laying them out in symmetrical piles, ready for the morning. He attends to his bathroom activities, such as brushing his teeth, combing his hair, titivating and generally admiring himself, and because he is so driven by routine, would never dream of leaving out a single step. He has recently added the process of shaving to his bathroom repertoire. He also has certain chores at home, such as setting the table for meals and clearing away afterwards. He is in charge of pouring drinks during dinnertime and does it with care and concentration, never spilling a drop. He closes all the curtains every night and turns on the lights. For the past five years, he has never once had to be told to go to bed. Every evening he puts on his pyjamas, brushes his teeth and kisses us all goodnight before turning in.

Jonathan does not have a clear understanding of the concept of danger, which is related to his trust and faith in humankind. I don't think he can grasp that there are people who would either purposely or accidentally do him harm. He still rushes forward without thinking of traffic danger. Although we have taught him not to dash away as he gets out of the car, he still gets enthusiastic about being somewhere familiar. He marches off, feeling very in control and independent, often walking quite far ahead of us. He has no fear that he could get lost or that we may not be there when he turns around. He has absolute faith in the fact that he knows what he is doing and that we will always be behind him. There has only been one incident where we lost Jonathan. We had gone to a large shopping centre to buy a suitcase when Jonathan was about eight years old. I was being shown various pieces of luggage and Barry was at the door with Jonathan, who sat down to feel the coarse texture of the mat at the door. A little later Barry was at my side making a comment about the luggage. I asked, 'Where's Jonathan?' We both looked towards the door and he was not there. He could dash away in the blink of an eye and it was uncanny that he was there one second and gone the next. It was a multilevel shopping centre crowded with Saturday shoppers. Barry and I both rushed off in different directions. At times like that you become oblivious to others and I was running along calling 'Jonathan' in the hope he would respond. I knew he would not respond, he never did, but I thought people around him would know that I had lost a child and point me in the right direction. We had taken Jonathan to a games arcade in the basement of that mall from time to time and, knowing Jonathan's uncanny sense of geography, I headed in that direction. There is nothing more frightening than losing a child who is not able to talk or understand danger. After much toing and froing from the luggage shop, which served as home base, I finally saw Barry coming towards me with Jonathan in his arms. It was a sight that made me happy and angry at the same time. Relief released anger and I could happily have throttled him there and then. Barry had found him in a CD shop very close to where we'd lost him, sitting flat on the floor doing the dance of joy while enjoying the music. Can you imagine how you would feel if you were choosing a CD and a big boy lumbered in, plonked himself down in the middle of the showroom floor, and started swinging his upper body vigorously from side to side, with his arms swaying around in the limited space? It does explain the shocked and confused faces Barry described. Only after my anger had subsided and my imagination stopped giving me violent scenarios of what could have happened to Jonathan, did I hold him and tell him how I didn't like it when I couldn't see him.

I often felt that the small gestures of letting Jonathan know how we were feeling were way over his head, but I don't think anything was wasted. When I see what he now takes in from information he is given, I realise that he has always absorbed more than I have given him credit for. Besides, if he hasn't benefited from the lectures I have given him, it has been cathartic for me and helped to dissipate my fears. It may sound as if I have always spoken quietly and in a controlled manner to Jonathan. This isn't true! He got very used to my shouting and ranting and the ongoing nagging, which is now seldom required. He has little lapses from time to time, usually from the excitement of having others around.

As Jonathan has become physically bigger, his behaviour often confuses others. His response to certain situations can be puzzling. The look of horror on Santa Claus's face last Christmas, as he saw a large man approaching to sit on his knee was a picture. He quickly realised that this six-footer was just a small boy with a Christmas wish, like all other small boys and played the role beautifully, despite crushed legs. This will probably be the last year that we will go to the Christmas displays in the big malls. Because of Jonathan's age it is important that we instil age-appropriate behaviour, but it is sad for me because I know that his mental age will always draw him to childish pleasures. It is very sad to see Jonathan head towards something that he would enjoy because of his mental age, his eyes dancing with excitement, and you know that his size is going to preclude him from the fun. It wasn't that long ago that Jonathan spotted a tiny plastic activity slide, probably meant for an eighteen-month-old baby, in a shop. His eyes lit up and he dashed towards it without considering that only one of his size ten shoes would be able to slide down it, provided it was taken off his foot. I often wonder how Jonathan perceives himself. We've often spotted him at his bathroom mirror, lost in admiration of his muscles and physique but, at the same time, we are reminded that intellectually he is still a small boy. It is with sadness that we realise he will always live in a world that is neither that of a man nor a boy. This was brought home the other day when Barry, Jonathan and I were driving along a main arterial road and passed a motor showroom with a huge blow-up Father Christmas at its entrance. Ten seconds earlier we had been travelling with a sedate and dignified adult looking studious in his spectacles in the back seat. In the blink of an eye he was replaced by an ecstatic four-year-old, clapping his hands and shrieking, 'Christmas, Christmas! Look, Santa Claus!' and launching into a high volume rendition of *Silent Night*.

Another painful reminder took place in an enclosed adventure park. Jonathan loved going there because it had a basketball hoop enclosure, surrounded by nets so that the ball could not bounce away. He is very good at shooting hoops and he played the game as if it was a televised Lakers match. That day I sat and had a cup of tea while I watched him play out his fantasy of team interaction with shouts of, 'Yes!', 'Give me five!' and 'Go, man!' When the big match was over, he decided to try some of the other equipment that really was a bit too small for him. He went into a netted area containing a mini trampoline. He was too big for the equipment, but was enjoying being there and no harm was being done. I had seen a few little girls in party dresses dashing to and fro, shrieking and running. As I watched them I overheard one say to the other, 'There he is, the monster, he's coming to get you. Run!' I felt wounded to the quick and the pain I felt was like a stab in the heart. I knew that this little boy was the furthest thing from a monster, and I also knew, thank goodness, that he would have totally missed the connotations of what they were saying, regarding it merely as a game. How I long for the day when all parents are educated enough to teach their children that people who are different are invariably harmless and only want to be friendly.

We have recently turned a fairly significant corner. Taking Jonathan to a doctor when he is sick has been a nightmare up to now. We needed to get a blood sample from Jonathan, having tried unsuccessfully twice before. His history in this regard is legendary. My regular doctor was not there, but her partner agreed to see him. A gentle lady called Belinda had promised to undertake the task. I spoke to Jonathan before we left home and said we were going to the doctor. After he'd said, 'Me? Me?' a few times, I assured him that it was him the doctor was going to see. He then said, 'Jon-Jon not sick.' I explained that she was going to draw blood. I waited for his response and he rolled up his sleeve and looked at the vein in the inside of his elbow. I said, 'I'll tell you what, if you let the doctor take blood and you are a good boy, I'll get you a juice and I'll take you to Granny and you can drink it there.' He said, 'Me? Granny? Juice?', looking interested. I waited with Jonathan, who was nursing his arm with the sleeve pulled up. When we got into the examination room, Belinda arrived and quietly explained to him that she was going to draw blood. She asked him to lie down and stood between him and the injection site, which was probably what made the procedure possible. I stood at the foot of the bed, babbling about Granny and juice and before we knew it, we had a tube of blood. It was such a breakthrough that my delighted reaction seemed to startle the staff. Jonathan looked over at me as Belinda was saying, 'Well done, Jonathan, you are such a big boy' and his face glowed with accomplishment. He got his juice, but didn't end up drinking it at Granny's house because of a fairly severe motor collision we had on the way there. My car couldn't be driven and was towed away, and we were taken home, very lucky to be unhurt.

Visits to the doctor were not always taken so seriously. When Jonathan was much smaller, in the grip of school holiday boredom, he wanted to go out in the car and nagged endlessly, bringing me my keys and handbag. I told him in no uncertain terms that we weren't going anywhere. He slunk off, seeming to accept this, but soon returned to tell me in a pathetic, but theatrical little voice, 'Jon-Jon sick – go doctor!' He apparently had great faith in his own powers of persuasion and would even risk a visit to the doctor for a drive in the car.

Chapter 25

There is often a particular occasion that marks the transition from childhood to young adulthood. It might be a matric farewell dance, a formal family occasion that requires dressing up, or seeing your child interacting socially in new situations. I have seen many girls transformed into chic debutantes and witnessed many boys becoming 'men about town', even if only for an evening. It is always a proud moment for parents to see their children dressed up and emulating their own social behaviour. It is usually a shock to see how grown-up their children become for the night, but starts the process of understanding that they have an independent adult in training.

It was a momentous occasion when Jonathan was invited to his first dance at school. We treated the occasion with the dignity it deserved and bought him appropriately smart clothes. He has seen his dad go off to work in a suit every working day of his life and I don't think it had occurred to him before that day that he could wear a jacket like his dad's. The new jacket was the highlight of his year.

The event started at six o'clock, but he would have been ready by two o'clock if he had had his own way. He had been for a haircut and I could not help thinking back to the days when he had to be held down to have one. Barry and I helped him shave and it reminded me of his mix of adult maturity and childish innocence. He bathed and dressed himself in the clothes he had set out in a neat row, in the order in which he would put them on. I caught him putting on some of Barry's aftershave and slapping his cheeks the way he had seen in a television commercial. Now all that remained was to put on his beloved new jacket. Barry took it off the hanger and Jonathan slipped his arms into it. His face split with a beaming smile that stretched from ear to ear. He looked at himself in total admiration and said, 'I carbelevit!' Well, we couldn't believe it either; the transformation was phenomenal. It seems that every time he puts on his jacket, he assumes a suave manner. He has adopted a behaviour code that matches his dress code. I'm sure it confirms what some psychologists say about labelling. If you call somebody a gentleman and treat them like one, they will act like one. Seeing the pride on Barry's face has engraved this special occasion on my heart forever. I looked at Jonathan; his Down syndrome characteristics were invisible to me, his speech seemed normal and he was the handsomest young man I had ever seen. Handsome means 'stately' and stately means 'of imposing appearance and manner'. That describes Jonathan perfectly that night. I felt an overwhelming sense of achievement on his behalf. He had been knocked down so many times and come back up to become the Jonathan who stood there in front of the mirror, proud and sure of himself with three pairs of adoring eyes on him, his own included.

We were due to pick him up at ten o'clock and arrived ten minutes early hoping to catch a glimpse of him having a good time and we did. He was dancing as if it was his night, all of the children there thought it was their night. There had not been too many occasions before that singled them out in their families and gave them an opportunity to feel the pride and excitement that dressing up brings. Jonathan came home exhausted and sweaty after hours of hectic disco dancing. It was evident that all the children had had a wonderful evening, partly fuelled by their lack of inhibition on the dance floor. Genetically normal children of this age are invariably fraught with insecurities about how they look and whether they fit in, so it's entirely possible that Jonathan and his friends had a far better time.

Graeme was away on a fishing trip that weekend and only due back the following evening. At four o'clock the next morning, Jonathan was at my bedside, fully dressed in the rumpled clothes he'd retrieved from the laundry basket, with his jacket on. He patted me on the cheek to wake me up and said, 'Show Graeme.' He stayed like that all of Sunday until Graeme got home and made an appropriate fuss of his smartly dressed brother.

When Graeme's car pulls into the garage, it is like pushing a button. Jonathan goes into action saying, 'Graeme, Graeme, I missed you!' He runs through the house towards the garage shouting, 'My brother, my brother.' Graeme normally leaps out of his car and shouts, 'Jonathan Wickins, what have you been doing, I've been missing you!' and Jonathan replies, 'Thanks Graeme,' as he hugs his brother around the chest. Their enthusiasm is absolutely mutual. Seeing each other again is always an occasion, even if it has only been an hour or two since they were last together. Both of them show the same delight in being reunited, so being separated for some time makes the reunion just that much more of a celebration. When Graeme is away from home, Jonathan often says, 'I miss Graeme' with longing in his eyes.

Jonathan does the same when Barry or I come home after being out. When Barry gets back from work he's made to feel welcome, but when he's been away for any length of time, he gets the red carpet treatment. Once, when Barry had been away overnight on a business trip, Jonathan flung his arms around Barry on his return, shouting, 'You're alive, you're alive! I missed you, Dad!' The 'alive' could only have been picked up from the movies or television, as it was so inappropriate. However, he knows exactly what 'I miss you' means and uses it a lot. He knows from his boarding school days that it is used when you first see someone after not seeing them for a while. He also knows that it is a compliment, having been on the other end of accepting it for so many years. Does he understand yearning? I think he does, but I don't think he knows it's called 'I miss you'.

'Look, Graeme, Dad's home!' Jonathan shouted. 'He was at the airport!' It has only recently become apparent that he thought that when people went to the airport, they remained there until it was time to come home. Once he had seen people boarding a plane, he realised that they actually left the airport building. However, it only occurred to me after that that he still harboured some serious misconceptions. He apparently believed that they remained in the plane, suspended in the atmosphere, until they touched down again. How I know this is that when my sister Pat returned to Panama after one of her trips home, every time Jonathan saw a plane overhead, for months afterwards, he looked up and waved shouting, 'Hello, Pat.' It is only since he has flown himself that he has realised that the purpose of boarding a plane is to reach a destination.

A pleasant ritual has developed around Barry's numerous business trips away from home. Every time he returns, it is Jonathan's self-appointed duty to bring Barry's briefcase and overnight bag from the car into the house. He first stashes the briefcase in its proper place in the study, and then unpacks the overnight bag, putting every item in its designated place. This routine is very important to him, as he views it as his responsibility. He often finds small tasks to do, which he executes meticulously and reliably, very unlike the average teenager.

Maintaining a daily routine has become easier as Jonathan has grown older. He conforms to rules and understands boundaries and accepts situations without question if you have said 'no'. We don't have 'Why not?' or 'My friends can.' It is only the unknown and unfamiliar that unhinges him. An unhinged Jonathan is not endearing, however. Patience needs to be mustered and stored for these refractory moments. The difficult times are usually associated with fear.

I am normally quite composed and easy-going, but there have been times when I have completely lost the plot. One of the more memorable occasions took place in a large and busy shopping mall, where Jonathan and I needed to get from one floor to the next. We had to use the elevator because of Jonathan's irrational, but very real, fear of a descending escalator and this was irritation number one for me. Before I could stop him, Jonathan had pushed both the 'up' and 'down' buttons for the elevator, which was irritation number two. The lift opened, crammed with people, and as Jonathan lurched forward to go inside, I realised the lift was going up. I yanked him back by the arm, saying, 'We'll wait for the next one, this one is going up.' Jonathan decided he was getting in regardless, probably thinking that I had changed my mind about the elevator and was planning to head for the escalator. We played tug of war between the bobbing doors of the lift for what seemed like an eternity, with a captive and stunned audience. If I had just followed him in, travelled to the top and come down again, I would not have been standing there with a rash on my neck, my hair wet from the battle, and humiliation seeping from every pore at the public spectacle we were creating. I am not usually stubborn, I can safely leave that to Barry, but if it had required a rugby tackle to get him out of the elevator, I was more than ready. Every parent will recognise the feeling. It usually starts with a relatively minor incident that becomes a major issue because of stubbornness. Instead of letting it go, one digs one's heels in as though defending one's honour, and ends up embarrassing only oneself.

Jonathan, being the mimic he is, creates both amusing and embarrassing times. I know I have to avoid people with a tic or physical impediment, because Jonathan starts flicking an eye or twitching his lip in identical fashion, unaware that it is not a game. In a bank queue not long ago, a husband and wife standing behind us were having a dispute. The wife's response was echoed by Jonathan, parrot-like, in the exact same whining nasal tone, 'Aah, give it a break!' I have become an expert at assuming a faraway and disconnected demeanour, pretending to be oblivious to what Jonathan has said or done. Thank goodness his speech is not very clear! The situation has improved as he has matured and we have taught him not to interact with strangers unless they make the first move. Before Jonathan understood this rule, he approached a dear old lady as she walked towards him, shuffling along with a walking stick. I would have assumed she would have trouble understanding his speech. She was bent over as she walked and Jonathan had to bend his knees to look into her eyes. Something told me this time that I should not pull him away. Unsure of what he was about to say, which could have been along the lines of 'May I use your walking stick?' or 'What is that hanging out of your ear?' referring to her hearing aid, I waited to see. Instead, I heard him ask solicitously, 'Are you tired? Is your leg sore?' She looked warmly at Jonathan and said, 'No, sweetheart, I'm not tired. I can even walk without my stick,' and she lifted the stick a few centimetres off the floor. They parted with Jonathan blowing kisses and me being terrified that we might have been the cause of a broken hip. She had responded so warmly to Jonathan, making me think she had perhaps met someone like him at some time in her long life.

There are experiences I hold dear, that I may never have had, but for Jonathan. I often think of his class gathered around a table, having lunch to celebrate one of his birthdays. There were usually about fourteen children from diverse cultures and backgrounds, with varying degrees of disability. Not one child would ever say, 'I don't like apple juice, I want orange' or 'I don't eat this.' They all ate and enjoyed what was put in front of them. Our children's exemplary behaviour always makes me proud, but never more so than on a particular occasion in a restaurant, where another of Jonathan's birthday parties was in progress. There was an adjacent table with a number of 'normal' children, also celebrating a birthday. I was forcibly struck by the sharp contrast between the two groups. One had been brought together by unfortunate circumstances, and were absolutely accepting of each other's limitations, while the other was characterised by flying food, shouting and unacceptably rowdy and bad behaviour. This proved again that IQ and good manners do not necessarily go hand in hand.

Chapter 26

Late one afternoon, the house was abnormally quiet. I went looking for Jonathan, calling from room to room, 'Jonathan, Jonathan', until his stern reply broke the silence, 'Don't call me names!' He had obviously heard some of his classmates saying this in a different context and liked how it sounded. Often Jonathan says things that have clearly been said in the classroom. Where else would he have learnt to point to his forehead with his finger and say, 'Think!' (or rather, 'fink!'), when he is not making himself understood and gets a blank stare? Where else would he have learnt 'You're not a baby, you're a senior' than in the senior phase at school? He reprimanded me recently with 'Don't walk away; you're a senior, not a baby!' I think I'd rather be called a baby!

Jonathan has a strong sense of humour and, together with his ability to mimic, he can be extremely amusing. Recently, on being offered something more to drink, he used a line from the popular television show, Mr Bean, saying, 'No, no, no, I'm driving!', the hand actions were perfect, the same deep, silly voice, and the sanctimonious face. He enjoys making us laugh and when he feels he's been successful, he really gets going. I have actually had someone chastise me for laughing at a joke he had made, saying I was cruel. As I've said before, there is a huge difference between laughing at his jokes and laughing at him derisively. On the contrary, not giving him the opportunity to show what he does best and enjoys most, would be cruel. Our home is usually filled with fun and he is usually at the centre of it. His rendition of the All Blacks' Haka would thrill anyone, not only a New Zealander.

He can be a tease when you least expect it. I asked him recently, as I often do, what his name was and he replied, 'Jon-Jon Wickins.'

I carried on: 'And your mom's name?'

'Liz Wickins.'

'What's your brother's name?'

'Graeme Wickins.'

'And your Dad's?'

'Bart Simpson!'

Young, small, yellow and foul-mouthed – somehow I don't think so. This entire exchange was conducted completely deadpan until the last line, when his eyes flickered in my direction to see if I had caught the joke.

With Jonathan's happy and uncomplicated personality, unaffected by scrutiny or judgement, it is surprising to me that he is afraid and threatened by certain things. He has a phobic fear of unfamiliar surroundings. His hands shake, he looks terrified and has even on occasion wet his pants. It is impossible to know how or why these phobias develop. Can we comprehend feeling that threatened? It is difficult to know whether to avoid or encourage these situations. In other words, do we dangle the carrot in front of his face to the ice cream stall and distract him until he no longer feels threatened, albeit with wet pants, or do we go home and comfort ourselves with the fact that he is emotionally intact? I prefer the wet pants option, perhaps because I know that everything Jonathan has achieved he has needed to go through that same process, feeling afraid until he realises there is no threat. Haircuts, horse riding, ice skating, even swallowing, are prime examples. They all happened with some trauma, but with plenty of encouragement. I would opt for the 'go home' alternative if Jonathan was embarrassed by a wet patch on his pants, but he couldn't give a hoot, and even less so if there is an ice cream involved.

Embarrassment is a concept that is probably too abstract for Jonathan to comprehend, along with modesty and inhibition. The incident below clearly demonstrates the difficulties connected to a grown-up body being steered by a child's mind, but is also a warning not to accept things at face value.

I was sitting at my computer and Jonathan flashed by the window without a stitch of clothing on, holding the clothes he had discarded in his arms. I was horrified and ran out of the closest exit into the garden after him. He had dropped a few items of clothing along the way, which I picked up; I had a shoe under my arm and a belt in my hand. Can you imagine what the neighbours would have thought if they had seen him running past the gate, across the driveway with no clothes on and me running after him with a belt in my hand? Later I pieced together how this situation had come about. I had watered the plants on the patio and Jonathan had obviously sat down, to do the dance of joy, in a pool of water that had drained from one of the pots. Like his father, he feels that discomfort needs to be addressed immediately, and taking off his wet clothes seemed, to Jonathan, a way of addressing it.

Modesty is a difficult concept to explain and it is more likely to be learnt by example than by explanation. Lately Jonathan wears a towel around his waist after a shower, often looking down on it with pride as he explains, 'Like Graeme.' He closes the door of his room and dresses in privacy now, hopping behind his cupboard door if he's caught unaware. A far cry from the flasher of a year ago!

Jonathan is very quick to apologise when he knows he has done wrong. I clearly have insisted on it too aggressively, because if I haven't understood what he has said and ask 'What did you say?', he either says 'Sorry' or 'Thank you'. Denial works for him when he is in a tight spot. When he has said or done something that is unacceptable and I question him, he says indignantly, 'Not me!' He recently decided to take six brand new birthday cards from my desk, which I had bought for upcoming family birthdays and addressed them to his imaginary friends. He was signing cards and scribbling on the envelopes, singing 'Happy Birthday' when I came into the room. He saw the wrath on my face and said, 'Not me!' I was reasonably sure that it was him holding the pen and writing 'J O O N H T N'. He darted into his bedroom, closed the door and braced himself for the inevitable.

Jonathan does not know about envy. Relationships with

213

people who do not resent you for your possessions or personal attributes are sincere and uncluttered. It shows a true love of others not to want what they have.

Because children with Down syndrome learn from the responses they get from the people around them, they find out very quickly how to push the right buttons to get a desired reaction. This makes them manipulative, if you allow it. I know that if I had allowed Jonathan to use that power, he would have abused it.

A classic example of unacceptable learnt behaviour was provided by an angelic-looking little girl with Down syndrome sitting high up on top of the jungle gym at her school. Everyone coming through the gate was greeted with a torrent of foul language. This does not fit the stereotypical picture many have in their minds of Down syndrome children being 'heaven's children'. It does, however, support the fact that she had been taught by example, particularly the tone, perhaps by a parent who had been pushed to the edge by the child. That parent now lives with the humiliation of the general assumption that this is the way they talk at home. Living with someone who parrots one's every move can be limiting and inhibiting. One dare not burp or do anything worse unless one wants it set for life as appropriate behaviour in all circumstances. Jonathan would not understand that this behaviour is okay in his bedroom, but not acceptable in church. Don't think, either, that you would get away with similar indiscretions in his presence. He's astute and vigilant and would blow your cover in a flash, with loud and theatrical protestations. If he was caught in the same position, however, it would not be regarded by him as a display of bad manners, but rather as the joke of the century. Jonathan was with me in a shop recently when a couple walked in with a baby. The air was redolent, causing the father to hold the mite up and sniff at its nappy while the mother said, 'Yes, she definitely needs a change.' I avoided all eye contact and made a beeline for the door, gasping for fresh air myself and dragging Jonathan with me. I am not sure which I feared most; Jonathan protesting loudly or admitting to it being him.

Jonathan can be a regular 'keeper of the morals'. He gets a distinctly sanctimonious and accusatory look on his face when he says, 'I don't lygit!' and when he's heard a rude word he scowls, 'Very rood!' And that's from a boy who recently called the headmistress a cow! I have noticed that the worst insults Jonathan could ever bestow, from the time he was very young, are somehow connected to the farmyard; a cow, a pig, a dog or a baboon. He used to say 'gog', before he could pronounce dog, in a very cutting way under his breath, together with a filthy look when he had no other form of defence. 'Pig' lost its sting with the advent of the popular movie *Babe*.

Although he is capable of being just as naughty as any other child, it is never with malice or vindictiveness. It is my belief that people with Down syndrome are incapable of real sin. Jonathan has, however, tested this theory from time to time. I don't think that thought popped into my head the day Jonathan locked the bathroom door, turned on the hand shower and squealed with delight as the shower snaked around uncontrollably and the water flooded out under the bathroom door into our bedroom. Turning the water on was not the crime: enjoying it and refusing to unlock the door was. He did not turn the shower on intending to flood the bathroom, but the bath tap was open and he bumped the lever that engages the shower. We called him through the bathroom window to pass us the key or open the door, but to no avail. Barry was forced to break the lock of the door.

Locked doors started presenting new problems. It happened quite suddenly that Jonathan was able to turn the key in a door. The first few times it happened, it was written off to chance because he had previously been unable to do it. Experience quickly taught us to remove all keys from the doors in the house. One evening he disappeared into our bedroom, locking himself in and falling asleep on our bed. We could not stir him, no matter how loudly we called. Finally Barry resorted to prodding him with the handle of a long featherduster through the window. Confused as to what was happening when he eventually opened his eyes, he stood up and walked around our bedroom in robot fashion, still fast asleep, before settling back to sleep on the other side of the double bed, where he could not be reached. I had visions of the welfare department knocking on the door at any moment, having had reports from neighbours of possible child abuse. Our mood was now one of frustration and impatience, and we had to tape on an extension to the handle of the featherduster in order to reach him while we continued yelling. After what felt like hours, he suddenly got up, unlocked the door and went straight back to sleep in the same position, unaware of the pandemonium he had caused.

Keys held enormous fascination for Jonathan, which necessitated keeping them very much out of his reach. Until this rule became entrenched, we had a few incidents with missing keys. In some cases, the keys never reappeared, but in one case my bunch of car keys was found in the outside kitchen drain a few days later, obviously having being flung out of the kitchen window. It happened to be parents' day at Graeme's school and many different excuses would be tendered as to why parents could not make it. The keys in the drain story must have sounded particularly lame, I'm sure.

The fact that we were caught unawares from time to time by Jonathan's ability to do things is indicative of how he developed in fits and starts. He reached a plateau in behaviour quite often, and when we least expected it, he started doing new things. There was often a spurt of development, then back to a plateau until the next surprise. As Jonathan would say, reciting AA Milne, 'Jonathan Jo has a mouth like an "O" and a wheelbarrow full of apprises.'

Despite the fact that Jonathan has no logic, he has an underlying aptitude for certain household mechanical and technical apparatus. He operates the electric gates and garage doors with precision, never making a mistake. I feel more comfortable when he is controlling the gates than when I am. He knows which keys open which doors, which is obviously very handy sometimes. He knows which television channels are assigned to which stations, and what their regular schedules are. He always knows what he has to wear to school on particular days. Some days it's a tracksuit for sports, other days it's his school tracksuit. He never forgets the day he has to take tuck money to school or to dress appropriately for a birthday party, and he always remembers the day he needs to take his drum to school. If ever I deviate from our usual routes, he never fails to ask where we are going. He recognises places we have been before. He still says 'Graeme swimming' when we go past Jilly's house. Jilly taught Graeme swimming ten years ago. I find it fascinating that he has been able to learn all this, but still can't recognise colours or manipulate numbers one to five, despite years of effort at home and at school.

He makes smart connections and associations. He is intuitive and emotionally sensitive. He knows to keep out of the way of people who are indifferent to him and to embrace the people who accept him.

For a large portion of Jonathan's early life, I envisaged feeding him porridge and trying to control his head swinging at his twenty-first birthday party. I'm thrilled to say that he will not be eating porridge or swinging his head, but I can't guarantee that he'll recognise the shape of the birthday cake or be able to count his own candles.

Chapter 27

I could never describe the monumental pride I felt when Jonathan's teacher gave me the news that he had been chosen among a group of seven children at the school to join the swimming team. This team was to train for a year and undergo stroke correction to be able to compete in an annual mile-long swimming marathon called the Midmar Mile.

I have to stress yet again that what parents of genetically normal children consider an accomplishment, we, as parents of disabled children, view as a miraculous triumph. Graeme had swum the Midmar Mile several times when he was at school. For him it was a challenge, but not the major triumph it would be for Jonathan. Graeme's ongoing strong level of achievement in all areas led us to presume that he would automatically also succeed as a swimmer. Jonathan's lack of academic achievement led us to presume that he would never excel at anything. The fact that he now swims far better than the majority of so-called normal people speaks volumes about what can be achieved.

Jonathan swam in various qualifying events before the Midmar Mile and to add to our joy of watching him swim these marathons, Graeme swam all of them with him. Each disabled swimmer needs a chaperone to swim alongside them while they participate in the various events and Graeme was once again at his brother's side.

I would never have guessed that Graeme and Jonathan's swimming pool fun over the years would have led to the opportunity for Jonathan to take part in something that has brought him and us so much pride and joy. Graeme did what he has always done – held back to allow Jonathan to shine. Graeme has had the ability to slow down his pace in all avenues of life to stay in line with his brother and this was a clear example of it.

Swimming together started when Graeme was about eleven years old. They played a game together in the pool which they called 'Marco Polo'. Graeme would call out 'Marco' and disappear under the water and Jonathan would try to dive down to catch him, his lifejacket keeping him afloat. Graeme would allow himself to be caught; and Jonathan would scream excitedly, 'Polo.' Jonathan would then wave a fist of triumph and shout, 'The winner!' Graeme reaped enormous joy from watching Jonathan believe he had won and the sense of accomplishment that was written on his brother's face. Jonathan's triumphs have brought Graeme more pleasure than his own. Many games like these were engineered to make Jonathan believe that he was better at them and had won.

We didn't know then that Jonathan's comfort in the water would lead to his being able to swim freestyle across a dam for forty-four minutes without stopping.

I can't help looking back over the years to the days when a

swimming pool meant huge trouble to me. I remember the days when I had nightmares about Jonathan's safety anywhere near water, as well as my irritation about our possessions being hurled over the swimming pool fence into the water. I also look back to the day when the doctor said to us, 'These children can cause problems at home – institutionalise him.' I have often asked myself how different our lives would have been if Jonathan had not come to us, either because our family had not been chosen or the doctor had been successful in persuading us to give him up. Our lives and values would be very different today. We sacrificed a normal existence in the early days and were constantly required to make allowances for Jonathan's inability to understand and conform. We all became accustomed to setting our needs aside to attend to Jonathan's, so we learnt to wait in queue for attention. How could we have known then that these sacrifices would reap such rewards and joy?

The day of the big swim arrived. It was a journey of several hundred kilometres to get to the Dam. The team members and their families met at the registration tent; the swimmers all dressed in their 'Casa Do Sol Aqua Team' jackets. The coaches had decided the previous week, and I agreed with them, that we would ask for a volunteer to swim with Graeme and Jonathan. Graeme wanted to be there to ensure his brother's safety and to encourage him but he is not capable of pushing Jonathan to the limit. His emotional bond with him does not allow him to be too firm or to force Jonathan into doing anything. We had watched Jonathan training and were certain that he could easily swim a mile. He was swimming it four times a week for months before the event. But if Jonathan could manipulate anyone, it would be Graeme, and we recognised that. In the previous qualifying swim, Jonathan had tried to climb on Graeme's back when the going got tough. If it wasn't for the fact that Jonathan is heavier than Graeme, Graeme may even have allowed it and carried him to the finish.

As we all gathered for the children to go down to the water's edge, it was announced over the loudspeaker that five volunteers were needed to accompany disabled swimmers. We were sent a wonderful young man called David who undertook the challenge. It was the perfect combination – one to encourage and understand Jonathan's speech and the other to coerce him across the dam. All we could offer David in the few minutes we had together before the race started was that he should keep insisting on 'long arms', Jonathan's understanding of freestyle swimming. Jonathan did his best time ever and finished the swim to great applause from the spectators. It may have had something to do with the fact that he raised his clenched fists skywards, punched the air, and shouted 'Yes!' several times as he ran up the ramp out of the water. The crowd loved it!

All seven of the children from the school completed the swim. The times ranged from thirty-three minutes by Colin, who also has Down syndrome, to Jonathan who did it in forty-four.

Barry and I were invited to the assembly at the school the next morning and Barry was asked to hand out the medals to the swimmers, which included two teachers who were the coaches and who swam with our children. I looked at the children on the stage that morning and marvelled at the fact that they had all had many challenges to overcome in their lives and yet they were ready to take on more. One of the swimmers is autistic and has no speech, two have Down syndrome and the others have varying types of learning disabilities. Did we ever think we would see them in a group with well-earned medals around their necks? It wasn't that long ago that we were saving Jonathan from bouncing off the walls and running wildly in unpredictable directions.

Jonathan's ability to swim and the training he has needed to do so has definitely improved his health. His previous poor muscle tone and respiratory problems have been immeasurably improved by this regime. His immune system has been strengthened by his general fitness, which is maintained by regular visits to the gym. I watch him when we are at the gym and wonder how he perceives himself within that sort of environment. It often strikes me how well he has adapted to fit into a normal world. I don't think he has the mental capacity to recognise that he is intellectually different to others. I believe he accepts everything at face value, his own level of functioning included. Someone asked me recently if I thought Jonathan felt trapped in a child's mind and longed to get out to function normally. I can truthfully say that I have never seen signs of anything other than Jonathan loving what he is. He is not able to assess how he would have functioned if he did not have Down syndrome or how others around him function by comparison. That is what makes most Down syndrome people so content; they like themselves and are completely complex-free, their facial expressions are usually testament to that. It is an enormous sadness when people with a mental disability are so mildly disabled that they know they are different. This must stem from the inevitable frustration of not functioning as others do. There may be some Down syndrome people who fit that category, but generally they don't.

As I stood at the fence watching all seven children run up the ramp after the race, I had an overwhelming feeling of pride. It felt like a lesson to everyone there that disabled people have value and are just as prepared to take on a challenge as anyone else.

To see the way Jonathan treasures his medals has made it all worth while. I watched him through the crack of the bathroom door while he admired himself in the mirror and gave what sounded like a victory speech with all four medals around his neck. As I was about to walk away I saw him lift one of the medals and kiss it. I decided to disappear quietly and overlook his lack of humility because I thought he had every reason to be proud.

Chapter 28

There have been many times in the last eighteen years that I have looked at Jonathan and believed with all my being that there was a purpose for him being sent to us. He has enriched our lives, made us more compassionate and better human beings, and given us the ability to love unconditionally. Graeme has fulfilled all our hopes and dreams of traditional parenthood and our love for him has been further enriched as he's shared our deep and committed love for Jonathan, never feeling threatened by it. If you have more than one child, you will know the feeling of witnessing loving interaction between them. That feeling is magnified a thousandfold when one of the children is disabled.

As I wrote this book, I tried to imagine what it would have been like if Jonathan had been born genetically normal. I have not been able to, not because I haven't wanted to, but because Jonathan is so unique that I cannot imagine him any other way. I have not been able to erase the slanty eyes and stubby fingers and substitute them with anything else in my attempt to imagine. I can't imagine him saying anything worse than 'cow' to anybody. My common sense doesn't allow me to play the futile 'what if' game, because I would have to wipe out so many things that have been meaningful to me and I can't. How could I pretend 'I carbelivit!' didn't happen? Him being chosen for first team rugby or as head boy would have made me no more proud than I was on the night of the St John's festival.

Some would say that a better choice, if given it, would have been to abort the pregnancy. Would Down syndrome have been reason enough to get rid of him? No! Jonathan has given us joy beyond measure. He has bonded us as a family in a way that is indestructible. We have loved each other for loving and accepting him. There are some things in life that you cannot change, so you learn to accept them until you no longer want them to be changed.

You will know from what you have read that we have had agonising decisions to make and times that were fraught with worry, but perhaps that is why we are so happy with what we have today. As I wrote the chapters filled with hardship and pain, I knew there was a happy ending to my story. I knew that everything I described would make you understand how our love for Jonathan became so powerful.

The story of Jonathan's journey would not be complete without mentioning the future. I have experienced waves of despair about what would happen to Jonathan if something should happen to us. It is any parent's worst nightmare, but becomes that much more upsetting when the child is not, and never will be, independent. There have been countless times when I've cried myself to sleep over who would give Jonathan his Marmite sandwich, who would take the trouble to cut his fingernails, and tuck him into bed if we were no longer here to do it for him. As the years have passed and Jonathan has become more self-sufficient, these desperate feelings have dissipated. I've learnt that it is an exercise in futility to worry about things that may never happen. We cling precariously to life and are sometimes forcefully reminded of how uncertain it can be. A car accident, no matter how minor, brings to mind what could happen. You acknowledge the lives that have been lost under similar circumstances by unlucky timing and wonder if it will happen to you because you no longer feel exempt. You realise that your life and your family's could change forever in a matter of seconds.

A way to ease the concern of leaving a child, in the event of your death, is to make suitable arrangements. I would be plagued with anxiety if there was not a financial plan for Jonathan or a suitable solution for his care in our absence. We have recently had to face the thought-provoking task of updating our wills, but it is another step towards knowing that we have done everything we can possibly do, while we are alive, to make provision for the event of our death. There are certain things that are within our control and others that are not. All we can do is to take responsibility for the things we can control. Jonathan has come close to death many times in the past eighteen years, so perhaps our concerns should include how we would cope without him, rather than how he would cope without us.

I don't think it was ever the intention that active parenthood should last for the rest of our lives. There comes a time for a son or daughter to move on to lives that no longer include us. For disabled people, that time of letting go is even more important. It is not a time I am looking forward to, but one I know I will need to face. How cruel it would be to keep Jonathan at home until we are too old to care adequately for him or attend to his needs. How cruel that, in the event of our death, Jonathan would have to cope with moving to a new environment, while at the same time suffering traumatic grief that he could not understand. We are in the fortunate situation of having access to a respite care facility every Saturday. Jonathan loves going there and it is an important part of his social life. He loves the group sporting activities and the routine that is always adhered to. It is Barry's and my day together, without guilt, because Jonathan longs for Saturdays. He wakes up at about four thirty in the morning, gets suitably dressed for an action-filled day, peaked cap and all, and waits patiently until nine o'clock. This is phase one of the transition that will be needed in due course. I can't see us being ready for it for some time, but slowly Jonathan will realise that life is not threatening without us. We will find that letting go will be easier when we've had some practice too. Instead of waking up one day and finding him gone forever, I would choose for the transition to be slow; so slow, in fact, that Jonathan will find it hard to tell which place he considers home.

Barry has, until now, held an idealised vision of Jonathan's future. He imagined a career for Jonathan, and building a separate cottage on our property for him to live in. He talked about Jonathan doing woodwork as a hobby and having his own workshop. I would love to think that Jonathan is going to be able to function independently, and I know I have said 'never say never' before, but it seems very unlikely. His continued social development will change him over the years and we cannot predict the extent of his development. His social and vocational needs will dictate what decisions will be made about his future when the time comes.

Knowing Jonathan as I do, I know that he would love to have a function of his own or a role to play, and would treasure it as his own purpose in life. He would be reliable in getting a task done and would not get bored with doing it day after day. I know he would see it as a new challenge every time he did it and feel the same self-worth and satisfaction that any of us get from the work we do.

Barry and I are starting to reach some common views as we watch Jonathan undertake new challenges and develop new skills from paying attention to the world around him. I can envisage him fitting in well and enjoying a workshop situation, making a career of it, and being able to experience employment and the self-esteem that goes with it. A workshop is usually an autonomous, non-profit facility that creates opportunities for employment for intellectually challenged youngsters. The concept is that the community provides simple and repetitive work for nominal wages, thereby engendering a sense of self-worth and participation in society. One of the great advantages of this system is that the youngster still lives at home, but his horizons have been greatly extended, preparing him for future independence.

We would like Jonathan to live at home with us while employed at a workshop, and at around twenty-four years of age we would have to assess the situation again. I have learnt, and I didn't learn it quickly or painlessly, that one should never try to predict what the future holds based on today's circumstances. Regular reappraisal of the situation reinforces my view that flexibility is the key. Because we are not able to know what development will take place, the best option is a wait and see approach. Should he eventually have to live in an adult care facility, for the first time in his life, I feel confident that he would cope admirably. With his newfound maturity has come a self-sufficiency that is enormously comforting to us.

No two families are alike in the way they function. Some have their focus on success and believe they are happy as long as everyone in the family is achieving. Other families focus on happiness, and place more importance on emotional stability than on achievement. There is no right way. All families are made up of individuals and all individuals are unique. If we were all the same, it would be possible and easy to have handbooks on how to do it all correctly. What is desirable to one person can be another's disappointment. The same applies to the families of disabled children. Some want to bring their child as close as possible to what they consider normal, at any cost to the child or family, while others want to get on with their lives as though nothing had changed. I have seen many families who overcompensate for their child's disability by tolerating unacceptable behaviour, to the point that they lose control altogether. You might be thinking after what I've told you about Jonathan's earlier behaviour, that I might be one of them. I am not. There is a difference between not being able to get through to a child in order to exercise control, and losing control through bowing to pressure from the child or taking the path of least resistance. It is hard for onlookers to make that distinction, but it is very real and often misunderstood.

People regularly tell me that I have been specially chosen as Jonathan's mother. 'Special children go to special parents', they say. I always accept it as a great compliment, but acknowledge that there are far too many special children abandoned by 'special' parents who didn't want them. If a group of 'normal' parents stood alongside a group of 'disabled' parents, one would not be able to tell them apart physically. However, there are vast differences. The 'disabled' parents have learnt to take any given situation and make the most of it. It was never in their plan that they would have little choice about where their children would go to school, or that the task of parenting would require so much personal effort, both physically and emotionally. They would never take anything their children are able to do, not matter how insignificant it may appear, for granted. Even the smallest advance is cause for renewed hope and celebration. The parents of genetically normal children can never understand the intensity of joy and pride that even the smallest accomplishment can bring. Their own children will develop within given parameters that are easily recognised. The joy that they experience when their children reach expected milestones is intensified a thousandfold for parents who have no guidelines or expectations.

When one falls prey to indifference or dissatisfaction, the cure is to take a good look around you. Inevitably, you will find many people worse off than yourself and find reason to be happy with what you have got. They say that if everyone threw their problems up in the air, it would be their own they would choose to catch. I know I would want mine because I understand them. Does that not say something about being sent what you can cope with?

There is a picture in my mind that I often use as a frame of reference. When I was desperately looking for a school to accept Jonathan just before he was sent to boarding school, I visited a local school in the hope that it would be suitable for Jonathan. Because of the gravity of the situation, I was in an unhappy frame of mind the day they walked me from class to class showing me their facilities. I went into the classroom of the more profoundly disabled children, who were in the middle of a music session. The music teacher was playing the piano and the children were singing. My eyes locked onto a boy in a wheelchair who was badly affected by cerebral palsy. His limbs were gnarled and clumsy, and he could not speak but he was responding to the song 'If you're happy and you know it clap your hands' by trying to clap his hands together without too much success. His eyes were shining with excitement and his smile, however skew, was beaming. I knew, as he knew, he was happy. I have recalled that moment over and over in my mind when things have gone wrong and have asked myself, 'If he can be happy, why can't I?'

We've all been taught not to stare at disabled people, but next time take a compassionate look because beauty can be found in the most unlikely places if we're free enough in our minds and hearts to look for it.

This poem was given to me by a friend who had lost her disabled child just a few months earlier:

Heaven's Special Child
By Edna Massionilla
Dedicated to parents of handicapped children

A meeting was held quite far from earth
It's time again for another birth
Said the angels to the Lord above
This special child will need much love

His progress may seem very slow
Accomplishments he may not know
And he'll require extra care
From the folk he meets down there

He may not run or laugh or play
His thoughts may seem quite far away
In many ways he won't adapt
And he'll be known as 'handicapped'

So let's be careful where he's sent
We want his life to be content
Please Lord find the parents who
Will do a special job for you

They will not realise right away
The leading role they are asked to play
But with this child sent from above
Comes stronger faith and richer love

And soon they'll know the privilege given
In caring for the gift from heaven
Their precious child so meek and mild
Is 'Heaven's Very Special Child'